The Salem Witch Trials

The Salem Witch Trials

Sandy Asirvatham

CHELSEA HOUSE PUBLISHERS
Philadelphia

Frontispiece: A melodramatic scene from the Salem witch trials depicts an accused woman appealing to Satan to save her.

CHELSEA HOUSE PUBLISHERS

Editor in Chief Sally Cheney
Director of Production Kim Shinners
Production Manager Pamela Loos
Art Director Sara Davis
Production Editor Diann Grasse

Staff for THE SALEM WITCH TRIALS

Senior Editor John Ziff
Assistant Editor Rob Quinn
Layout by 21st Century Publishing and Communications, Inc.

© 2002 by Chelsea House Publishers, a subsidiary of Haights Cross Communications, LLC. All rights reserved. Printed and bound in the United States of America.

First Printing

1 3 5 7 9 8 6 4 2

The Chelsea House World Wide Web address is
http://www.chelseahouse.com

CIP applied for ISBN 0-7910-6328-3

Contents

GREAT DISASTERS
REFORMS and RAMIFICATIONS

Jill McCaffrey
National Chairman
Armed Forces Emergency Services
American Red Cross

Introduction

Disasters have always been a source of fascination and awe. Tales of a great flood that nearly wipes out all life are among humanity's oldest recorded stories, dating at least from the second millennium B.C., and they appear in cultures from the Middle East to the Arctic Circle to the southernmost tip of South America and the islands of Polynesia. Typically gods are at the center of these ancient disaster tales—which is perhaps not too surprising, given the fact that the tales originated during a time when human beings were at the mercy of natural forces they did not understand.

To a great extent, we still are at the mercy of nature, as anyone who reads the newspapers or watches nightly news broadcasts can attest.

Hurricanes, earthquakes, tornados, wildfires, and floods continue to exact a heavy toll in suffering and death, despite our considerable knowledge of the workings of the physical world. If science has offered only limited protection from the consequences of natural disasters, it has in no way diminished our fascination with them. Perhaps that's because the scale and power of natural disasters force us as individuals to confront our relatively insignificant place in the physical world and remind us of the fragility and transience of our lives. Perhaps it's because we can imagine ourselves in the midst of dire circumstances and wonder how we would respond. Perhaps it's because disasters seem to bring out the best and worst instincts of humanity: altruism and selfishness, courage and cowardice, generosity and greed.

As one of the national chairmen of the American Red Cross, a humanitarian organization that provides relief for victims of disasters, I have had the privilege of seeing some of humanity's best instincts. I have witnessed communities pulling together in the face of trauma; I have seen thousands of people answer the call to help total strangers in their time of need.

Of course, helping victims after a tragedy is not the only way, or even the best way, to deal with disaster. In many cases planning and preparation can minimize damage and loss of life—or even avoid a disaster entirely. For, as history repeatedly shows, many disasters are caused not by nature but by human folly, shortsightedness, and unethical conduct. For example, when a land developer wanted to create a lake for his exclusive resort club in Pennsylvania's Allegheny Mountains in 1880, he ignored expert warnings and cut corners in reconstructing an earthen dam. On May 31, 1889, the dam gave way, unleashing 20 million tons of water on the towns below. The Johnstown Flood, the deadliest in American history, claimed more than 2,200 lives. Greed and negligence would figure prominently in the Triangle Shirtwaist Company fire in 1911. Deplorable conditions in the garment sweatshop, along with a failure to give any thought to the safety of workers, led to the tragic deaths of 146 persons. Technology outstripped wisdom only a year later, when the designers of the luxury liner *Titanic* smugly declared their state-of-the-art ship "unsinkable," seeing no need to provide lifeboat capacity for everyone onboard. On the night of April 14, 1912, more than 1,500 passengers and crew paid for this hubris with their lives after the ship collided with an iceberg and sank. But human catastrophes aren't always the unforeseen consequences of carelessness or folly. In the 1940s the leaders of Nazi Germany purposefully and systematically set out to exterminate all Jews, along with Gypsies, homosexuals, the mentally ill, and other so-called undesirables. More recently terrorists have targeted random members of society, blowing up airplanes and buildings in an effort to advance their political agendas.

The books in the GREAT DISASTERS: REFORMS AND RAMIFICATIONS series examine these and other famous disasters, natural and human made. They explain the causes of the disasters, describe in detail how events unfolded, and paint vivid portraits of the people caught up in dangerous circumstances. But these books are more than just accounts of what happened to whom and why. For they place the disasters in historical perspective, showing how people's attitudes and actions changed and detailing the steps society took in the wake of each calamity. And in the end, the most important lesson we can learn from any disaster—as well as the most fitting tribute to those who suffered and died—is how to avoid a repeat in the future.

Afflicted girls and women "see" specters in the air during the Salem witch trials. Though the Salem episode occurred more than three centuries ago, it retains a firm grip on the American imagination.

What Dorcas Good Suffered

About 50 years ago in the town of Salem, Massachusetts, construction workers digging at the site of a future telephone company office building on St. Peter Street uncovered an ancient stone-walled dungeon. Although the 17th-century structure had been obscured by successive generations of town buildings, and although it had been hiding quietly under the ever-changing, slowly urbanizing landscape for hundreds of years, a sensitive and historically aware observer at the unearthed site could easily imagine the horrors once suffered here. In this dark, damp, and bitterly cold place, the smells of human bodily wastes, sweat, and sheer terror would have commingled to produce an unbearable stench. Being close to a river, the dungeon was most likely a home for water rats, the kind that would have scuttled fearlessly and willy-nilly over chained, manacled prisoners. Such a place would have been a natural breeding ground for all manner of disease: deadly diseases, or merely agonizing ones that weren't polite enough to offer their sufferers an early release into death. Diseases of the psyche and soul as well as of the body.

Into this man-made hell-on-earth, a bewildered young girl named Dorcas Good was brought for two weeks, removed temporarily to be "examined" by local officials, then returned to the dungeon and chained to a wall for what must have seemed an eternity. She, along with her mother, Sarah, had been accused of making common cause with the Devil—of practicing the black art of witchcraft and using their skills to torture and torment their innocent neighbors. Sarah was an outcast in Salem Village, an argumentative, verbally abusive beggar-woman who had been considered a nuisance for many years previous. She denied all charges of witchcraft, but her daughter, under the severe duress of official examination, broke down and tearfully confessed.

Little Dorcas was four and a half years old. "No doubt," one historian has speculated,

> even in her . . . agony she was, at best, largely ignored by the adults around her. Distraught prisoners and cruel wardens lack the motive or impulse to care for a child. It is unlikely that even her mother had much love left to give her. A new baby she had brought into the prison had already died or was dying.
>
> Dorcas was to spend many months without seeing the light of the sun, unable to walk and with nothing to play with but the rags she was wearing. The little fingers that picked at and twisted and folded the torn, filthy cloth were the only part of her being she could move without hindrance or pain. At first she may have shouted and wept. Perhaps she banged her head on the wall she was chained to. But, like all small children without care, stimulation, or love, in the end she went silent, rocking to and fro, as far as her chains would allow, or lying still, staring blankly.

Dorcas spent eight months chained to the stone walls of the Salem Town prison. She emerged as a five-year-old broken spirit and grew into a crazed woman unable to care for herself and forever dependent on her penurious father. But because she had confessed, her life had been spared. Her mother, who refused to confess, had arguably suffered less in the end: not very long after losing her baby to the deadly cold and damp of the prison, Sarah Good was hanged.

The stone-walled dungeon uncovered in the 1950s

Four-year-old Dorcas Good was chained to the walls of this dank, dark "witch gaol" for eight months. The experience left her mentally unbalanced for the rest of her life.

was only one of the several terrifying, soul-killing prisons where the accused would have been locked up during the witch hysteria that engulfed Salem and its neighboring communities in 1692 and 1693. Over the course of about 18 months, nearly 150 Puritans—mostly residents of Salem Village (a small and relatively rural annex of the larger Salem Town) and nearby Andover—were apprehended for using ungodly supernatural powers to torment and sicken their relatives and neighbors. Their chief accusers at the beginning were girls between the ages of 9 and 20, but this chorus of young "afflicted" females was supported and soon joined by several adult accusers, both men and women. Under a specially convened court, in open view of their accusers and the entire Salem Village community, the alleged witches—at first just a few elderly or outcast women, but ultimately a whole host of men, women, and children of all ages and from all social classes—were subjected to a swift and inexorable trial process that simply presumed they were guilty from the start. (The legal concept of "innocent until proven guilty" would not become formally established in America until the late 18th century.) Those who confessed were spared their lives. Those who denied the charges were clapped in chains and sentenced to die. In the end, 19 of the convicted witches were hanged, while one particularly unlucky soul, an old man in his eighties, was "pressed" to death—slowly suffocated as his executioner placed a mound of heavy rocks on his chest, one by one. Four other people died in jail before reaching trial.

After higher authorities intervened to put an end to the witch-hunt, the majority of convicted persons were eventually released from prison. But they escaped execution only to find their property confiscated, their families torn asunder, their ties to their neighbors severed, and their faith in human decency irrevocably damaged, if not shattered altogether. Years later, many of the people involved in the rounding up and conviction of the Salem witches—court officials, jury members, and (most notably) one of the "afflicted" girls herself—would come forward in contrition, fearing that their panic and misjudgment had helped destroy innocent lives.

This tragic episode is one of the most infamous and most heavily researched events in early American history, and yet it remains a frighteningly mysterious tale. Despite the work of dozens of historians over the ages—who have relied on a wealth of first-hand documentary evidence concerning the trials—the "ultimate truth" of the event is still obscured by debatable analyses and unanswerable questions. Were the young girls who first showed signs of being "afflicted" by witches simply faking, or were they in the thrall of a genuine collective delusion? Is it possible that an actual physical ailment was the root cause of their sufferings, which they later blamed on sorcery? Were the adults who believed the accusers merely Satan-fearing churchgoers who had only the best intentions to save their community from devilry—or were they coconspirators using the witch panic as a convenient cover for personal and political gain? What was the true role of Tituba, the slave who was (depending on which source you consult) either an Arawak Indian or a black African or some mixture of Indian and African, and who may or may not have practiced folk magic from her country of origin? Was Samuel Parris—the argumentative preacher and father of the first afflicted girl, Betty—a victim, a misguided victimizer, or an outright villain? Finally, is it possible that witchcraft was indeed being practiced in Salem, thereby justifying the initial panic?

Every generation of scholars and writers brings fresh interpretations, but these are supplanted eventually by later attempts to explain "definitively" what happened.

And although the basic facts of the episode are beyond dispute, new information about the trials may still be out there, hidden from view, awaiting discovery at a construction site or moldering in an attic somewhere in New England. As recently as 1999 some previously unknown documents surfaced and a new name was added to the list of those formerly arrested and charged with witchcraft.

In terms of the number of lives lost or destroyed, the Salem witch-hunt was a relatively minor episode compared with its historical precedents. Over a period of 300 years in medieval and early Renaissance Europe, *hundreds of thousands* of alleged witches were accused, tried, sentenced, and executed (usually burned alive at the stake) by the religious and political authorities of the time. Witchcraft, magic, sorcery, shamanism, witch doctoring—the history of human culture and religion is permeated by various attempts to summon supernatural forces for good or evil purposes. The relationship between officially sanctioned religious rituals and "grass-roots" witchcraft practices varies from era to era and from culture to culture. In the early centuries of Christian Europe, church leaders were fairly tolerant of folk-magic practitioners (for example, village "wise women" who proffered potions to cure illnesses or generate good luck or spark a romance). Toward the 13th and 14th centuries, however, this tolerant attitude was supplanted by a growing fear that witches were actually servants of the Devil.

People had generally always believed in Satan or the Devil, and thought of him as a powerful, active, malevolent force, capable of appearing in personal form to tempt the innocent, as he had done with Jesus Christ. But because of a number of complex historical and philosophical developments in this period, Christianity had become even more rigidly dualistic, focused on a stark and ongoing battle between the forces of good and evil. In medieval cosmology,

there were no such things as accidents—all human events had their originating cause in either the Lord or his Eternal Enemy. Therefore, it made perfect sense to blame any bad occurrence (the death of a child, the failure of a crop, and so on) on Satan and his disciples—witches.

Witch-hunts grew prevalent among all Christian denominations, including Protestants and Calvinists. But it was the Inquisition—a unified, long-standing endeavor of the Roman Catholic Church to purge its ranks of heretics and all other enemies of Christ—that raised the witch-hunt to a form of macabre science. Using a terrifying and inflammatory manual called *Malleus Maleficarum* (The Hammer of Witches) as their guide, the inquisitors broadcast stories of witches who performed terrible satanic and sexual transgressions, striking fear in the hearts of common people and encouraging them to

This 16th-century wood engraving depicts suspected witches being burned at the stake in Europe. By the late 17th century, at the time of the Salem hysteria, witch-hunts in the Old World had become quite rare.

Fire and the wheel: one Inquisition method for extracting a confession. For centuries, torture had been an accepted investigative tool, and the concept that the accused might have certain rights was unknown.

inform against one another. Accused persons were tortured until they confessed, and confessed witches were then executed. Most of the accused were women, for it was women who had traditionally practiced common folk magic. (And women, it was generally believed, are fundamentally weak and therefore especially susceptible to being seduced and recruited by the Devil.) Professional witch-finders identified and tested suspects for "evidence" of witchcraft—for example, some unusual growth or mole on the body that seemed insensitive to pain, thought to be Satan's mark—and collected fees for each successful conviction. Young children were often the victims of witch-hunts, but they also began to play a frighteningly predominant role in the accusation of witches—a pattern repeated at Salem.

During the Renaissance (15th and 16th centuries), the rise of a scientific, rationalist, humanist view of the world in some quarters caused a backlash among those with more orthodox beliefs, inciting a fresh wave of witch crazes throughout Europe. The persecution of witches significantly declined in the Old World during the 17th century and was almost unknown by about 1700. Salem, Massachusetts, circa 1692 was, therefore, a very late episode of witch hysteria—a throwback to a much earlier time.

A small number of victims, and a late date of occurrence: why, then, has Salem lodged in the American popular imagination as firmly as our mythical (and rather inaccurate) image of the Pilgrims' first Thanksgiving? Various historians have argued that the Salem episode can be seen as a pivotal, defining moment in early American history. As one writer put it, the trials "were a turning point in the transition from Puritanism, with its values of community, simplicity, and piety, to the new Yankee world of individualism, urbanity, and freedom of conscience." Just as the conflicts between scientific rationalism and traditional religion helped create the conditions for witch panics in early Renaissance Europe, another kind of culture clash here in the New World was responsible, in part, for what happened in Salem.

But more to the point, the small scale of the Salem story is exactly what makes it "manageable" by our collective memory. To read through the first-hand documents—the trial transcripts, journal entries, letters, and journalistic reports by credulous or skeptical observers—is to be immersed in a very vivid drama involving well-drawn individual personalities and a series of episodes that unfold step by step, day after day, over the course of just a few months. It is far easier to imagine the execution of 20 people, during one year in one small Massachusetts town, than to fathom the hundreds of thousands who perished in similar episodes all over the European landscape over the course of centuries. It may not be possible to feel genuine anguish over the fates of countless old women who died 500 years ago, but it is certainly possible to sympathize with the horrid abuse of a four-year-old girl named Dorcas, caught in the wheels of a communal disaster.

Salem is a specific story about a specific time and place, but it is also a symbol. Its well-documented trials "provide an astonishingly clear and instructive model of the universal and timeless processes by which groups of human beings instigate, justify, and escalate persecution," one historian has observed. Cautionary tales rarely come in such neat packages, but how well has caution been heeded? The fear of personified evil—the belief that some form of devil can take human form and recruit willing human servants to do his dirty work—has never gone completely out of style, even if it travels under different names. In the 1950s in this country, growing fear of communism led to a panic in which many persons were accused, on little or no evidence, of being Soviet spies.

Many lives were ruined. Historians still debate whether the panic was justified or outrageous, and whether the accused Soviet sympathizers were innocent victims of hysterical politics, genuine traitors, or something in between. In more recent years, children have once again played a starring role in disastrous episodes of alleged "satanic ritual abuse" by parents or caretakers. Despite the distance of 300 years, a number of disturbing similarities can be seen between these cases and the Salem episode—particularly in the willingness of authorities to coerce confessions and to believe the most bizarre and gory tales of torture and killing

(continued on page 24)

ARTHUR MILLER'S *THE CRUCIBLE*

Beginning in the late 1940s, Americans got caught up in a widespread panic about a different sort of "red devil": Communists. Although the capitalist and democratic United States and the Communist and totalitarian Soviet Union had been uneasy allies during World War II, after the defeat of Nazi Germany the relationship between the two nations became increasingly strained. Through forced occupation, the Soviets had set up Communist governments in many countries of Eastern Europe, and their apparent intention was eventually to export communism to the rest of the world—through almost any means available. The United States, by contrast, stood ready to oppose the spread of communism—also by almost any means. The struggle for influence between these two powerful adversaries led to the Cold War, a decades-long conflict fought through espionage and covert actions, hard-ball diplomacy, and proxy wars (wars involving allies of each nation).

In 1949, two shocking events convinced many Americans that the Soviet Union was getting the upper hand and the whole world was about to "go Red": a Communist named Mao Zedong took power in China; and the Soviet Union successfully tested an atomic bomb, ending America's monopoly on the most destructive weapon ever developed. In this climate of fear, many Americans were willing to abandon several of their nation's sacred principles—freedom of belief and freedom of expression—in the name of stopping Communist sympathizers at home.

In 1948, the U.S. House of Representatives had set up a special committee with the job of protecting the U.S. government from Communist infiltration. Headed by Senator Joseph McCarthy of Wisconsin, the House Committee on Un-American Activities (HUAC) instigated a nearly 20-year-long witch-hunt for Soviet spies and sympathizers among government workers, as well as among writers, entertainers, college professors, and members of other professions. McCarthy made widespread accusations based on rumors and speculative evidence. Many businesses and organizations began "blacklisting" accused Communists—barring them from working—even if there were no hard evidence against them. Accused persons were harassed into naming other Americans who might also be Communists. The committee was particularly vexed by alleged Communist influence in the Hollywood film industry. Many

From 1950 to 1954, Senator Joseph McCarthy (above) led a witch-hunt for Communists that ruined the careers of many innocent Americans. In the paranoid hysteria of the era, directly confronting McCarthy and his allies was impossible, so playwright Arthur Miller wrote about the Salem witchcraft trials in The Crucible. The historical parallels were obvious.

writers, producers, and actors were investigated and then, as a result, blacklisted by their colleagues in the business. Those who confessed and offered names of other offenders were usually allowed to continue working. Ten who refused to cooperate with the committee were ultimately imprisoned.

Many writers and intellectuals had noted disturbing similarities between the HUAC investigations and the Salem witch trials. Arthur Miller, a successful playwright who had won a Pulitzer Prize for his 1949 drama *Death of a Salesman*, was deeply troubled by McCarthy's zealotry and HUAC's power to destroy people's lives based on scant evidence of wrongdoing. In response, he wrote a play called *The Crucible*, nominally about the events of 1692 in Salem, but clearly referring to the present-day political atmosphere.

The play took many liberties with the actual history of the witch trials and should not be read as an accurate account. But it did go a long way toward capturing the fear, paranoia, greed, malice, unacknowledged sexual undertones, and general human frailty that must have characterized the actual event.

The first audiences to see *The Crucible* in 1952 were deeply offended and angered by the obvious parallels between past and present. How could Miller exploit such a glib analogy? they asked indignantly. Witches weren't real, but the threat from Communists was very real, they insisted. Yet the tide was already turning in a new direction. Politicians and journalists began openly questioning HUAC's heavy-handed methods and use of speculative evidence. Public opinion started turning against McCarthy, and in this atmosphere, audiences were more receptive to the historical comparison made by *The Crucible*. By 1954, Miller's play was an off-Broadway hit.

In 1956, having been "named" by an old friend who'd agreed to HUAC's demands, Miller himself appeared before the committee. He confessed to having harbored Communist sympathies when he was young, but said he had long since renounced those views. Miller refused to name other offenders, however, and was charged with contempt. Those charges were soon dropped.

Changing times eventually took the wind out of HUAC's sails. The committee, largely inactive through the 1960s, was finally dissolved in 1975.

In 1996, Miller was involved as a consultant during the production of the Hollywood film *The Crucible* (starring Daniel Day-Lewis and Winona Ryder). During that period, he recalled the weeks he'd spent, back in the 1950s,

> reading testimony by the tome, commentaries, broadsides, confessions, and accusations. And always the crucial damning event was the signing of one's name in "the Devil's book." This Faustian agreement to hand over one's soul to the dreaded Lord of Darkness was the ultimate insult to God. But what were these new inductees supposed to have *done* once they'd signed on? Nobody seems even to have thought to ask. But, of course, actions are as irrelevant during cultural and religious wars as they are in nightmares. The thing at issue is buried intentions—the secret allegiances of the alienated heart [are] always the main threat to the theocratic mind.

(continued from page 20)

without any physical or substantial evidence whatsoever.

And although the term *witch-hunt* has become a cliché—a commonplace way of describing almost any situation, no matter how serious or trivial, that involves a panicked but dubious search for alleged or actual wrongdoers—there are still cases in which the term applies quite literally. Consider, for example, a situation that occurred in 1988 in Jamestown, a small community in a sparsely populated region of north-western New York State. One historian of the Salem episode referred to the Jamestown story to show that these kinds of widespread "supernatural" panics can grow out of very mundane, worldly causes and quickly snowball:

> The region faced hard times; unemployment was rising; teen suicides seemed to point to a broader moral crisis. In the midst of these troubling conditions, an old warehouse was refurbished for use as a rock music concert hall and rented out to heavy metal musicians. At the same time, parents were watching network television shows that sensationalized stories of satanic worship. Rumors circulated among the teenagers through oral networks that were already established [i.e., through gossip]. Parents overheard bits and pieces of these reports and took their concerns to the police department in Jamestown. A group panic soon engulfed the community, centered on a tale that a blue-eyed, blond-haired teenage girl would soon be abducted and sacrificed in a satanic ritual. With slightly different details, the same story circulated in all the towns in the region. The episode died when authorities reassured parents that no such plot existed—but had authorities believed more strongly in the underlying mythos of abduction or the active interest of Satan in the [Jamestown area] towns, the result might have been different.

This anecdote should make one thing very clear: When we read about the witch trials that took place 300 years ago, we should not allow ourselves to feel intellectually or morally superior to the Puritans. We may not live our lives in constant fear that great forces of evil are lurking just outside the door, aided and abetted by distrustful neighbors or suspicious strangers. But the ancient fear persists inside us as individuals and as communities, and can emerge powerfully in times of great social stress. Clearly the suffering of a four-year-old accused witch named Dorcas Good—and many others—is not quite yesterday's news.

The Afflicted and the Accused

Two magistrates from Salem Town interrogate a witness and observe the fit of an afflicted girl during the early days of the witch hysteria. Fits that resembled epileptic seizures, along with trances, were the first "evidence" of witchcraft in Salem.

2

Cooped up in the house during the winter of 1691, nine-year-old Betty Parris and her cousin, 11-year-old Abigail Williams, took to playing fortune-telling games, a common though discouraged activity among young girls back then—and not unlike the kinds of playful supernaturalism (levitation, the telling of ghost stories, and so on) indulged in by preteens even today. They filled a cup with milk and an egg, looking in to discover clues about the men they might one day marry. As the story goes, instead of the images of their future husbands, they saw the shape of a coffin. It terrified them, although probably not because of its obvious association with death. Betty and Abigail would have seen plenty of real coffins in their time. As Salem witch trial historian Peter Charles

Hoffer observed:

> Death was very near all these girls. King William's War
> had made Salem a haven for refugees from French and
> Indian raids. Such a raid had carried off the parents and
> siblings of other girls their age. Epidemic diseases such as
> smallpox and typhoid regularly slaughtered the young.
> The Puritans had learned to prepare their children for
> death; indeed, they harped on the nearness of it.

For Betty and Abigail, the coffin's meaning was not so
much a threat of death, but a sign that they had violated
the rules for godly behavior—rules firmly established by
Puritan culture and reinforced very close to home, for
Betty's father and Abigail's uncle was Samuel Parris, the
preacher of Salem Village.

We will never know whether the vision of a coffin was
somehow a psychological catalyst or cause for the unusual
symptoms the girls later suffered, although some modern
historians are inclined to see things this way. All we have
are our suspicions, and the basic chronology of what happened next: A few weeks after the fortune-telling incident,
in January 1692, Betty fell strangely ill. She would slip into
trances, babble incoherently, scream and shriek, and fall
into what looked like epileptic fits. Soon after, Abigail,
who lived in the same house, started having the exact same
symptoms. After examining the girls, a local physician
named Dr. Griggs could come up with no natural medical
explanation for the girls' bizarre ailment. His learned
opinion, then, was that the girls were under an evil hand—
that their torments were of the Devil's making.

For the times, it was not a farfetched conjecture. The
Puritans—who had escaped persecution in their home
country of England by settling the Massachusetts Bay
Colony in the early part of the 17th century—believed
fervently in Satan's ability to cause misfortune through his

For the Puritans and for most Christians of the era, the existence of witches, agents of Satan, was assumed.

earthly agents, commonly known as witches. This belief was as strong among Harvard-trained ministers as among farmers, merchants, and common people—perhaps even stronger, for preachers often railed against witchcraft and devilry from the pulpit and in published treatises, in order to keep ordinary folks from slipping into skepticism or disbelief. After all, belief in Satan went hand in hand with belief in God. If you doubted the Devil's powers and willingness to interfere in human affairs, you may as well have declared yourself an atheist altogether. Among Puritans, who considered themselves God's chosen people, such a declaration was close to unthinkable.

Not long after Dr. Griggs gave his diagnosis, his own maidservant, 17-year-old Betty Hubbard, began suffering the same symptoms. The girls' fits came and went: periods of thrashing, screaming, and babbling were followed by utter calm and normalcy. Soon the ranks of sufferers expanded to include other young women in the neighborhood, including Ann Putnam, daughter of one of the most powerful men in town, Thomas Putnam.

In a widely read book about witchcraft, the New England church leader Cotton Mather had proposed prayer and fasting as the way to cure persons afflicted by witchcraft. Betty's father, Samuel Parris, was the pastor of Salem Village's church, and he used the power and visibility of his position to summon prayers from the church deacons and the entire congregation (probably close to 500 people). But the attempted cure was not working. The girls' fits continued.

Throughout history, people have sometimes turned to "white magic" or folk magic in an attempt to influence events in their favor or to counteract the harms wrought by the practitioners of "black magic," the Devil's disciples. To this day, there are those who practice some form of witchcraft as an alternative to organized religion. In some cultures and eras, witchcraft or folk magic can be seen as one way in which women and other relatively powerless individuals compensate for their lack of influence in "official" religious proceedings and practice. Puritans, especially women, had surreptitiously retained the culture of English folk magic despite the fact that influential church leaders frowned upon it. From the church's perspective, even "white magic" smacked of using the Devil's tools to defeat the Devil, and should therefore be feared and forbidden.

This was the atmosphere in which Mary Sibley, a member of Samuel Parris's church and one of his neighbors, decided to make use of an old English recipe for witch cake. Apparently without consulting Parris him-self, Mary Sibley approached Tituba—Parris's household slave, who had helped raise Betty and who was as anxious as the girl's parents to see her well again. Sibley claimed that the cake would help reveal the identity of the witch tormenting Betty and the other girls. Following Sibley's instructions, Tituba asked her husband, John Indian, to collect the children's urine, which was then mixed with rye flour and baked in ashes. The cake was then fed to a household dog. As an old English superstition held, the dog would then immediately run to the witch. But this attempt at counter-magic not only failed (the dog merely got sick from eating the cake), it backfired rather horri-bly. Reverend Parris learned about the witch cake, and the next Sunday he blasted Mary Sibley in front of the entire congregation for "going to the devil for help against the devil." Sibley was made to repent publicly, which she did with tears in her eyes and with a promise never to dabble in witchcraft again.

Although Sibley was never again accused of practicing the Devil's arts, her reliance on an old folk-magic remedy served to remind the Salem villagers that such practices did indeed go on in everyday life, despite the teachings of the church. The witch-cake episode hit a collective nerve, but it agitated Samuel Parris in particular. His daughter and the other afflicted girls, who had originally offered no explanation for their strange symptoms, had by this time absorbed the opinions of their elders. They now claimed that invisible agents were tormenting them—biting and pinching them, causing their limbs to twist this way and that in directions that seemed physically impossible. Parris went to the girls and demanded that they reveal the identity of those who had bewitched them. After some reluctance, they named Tituba—an astonishing identification, for Tituba had loved Betty as dearly as her own daughter.

Parris was dissatisfied (perhaps he believed a slave woman could not be intelligent or capable enough to cause such havoc on her own) and pressed the girls for more names. They soon obliged, offering the names of Sarah Osborne and Sarah Good, two village women.

In late February, Parris and Thomas Putnam urged two magistrates from Salem Town to come interrogate the accused witches. On March 1, the three women were arrested and brought to Ingersoll's Tavern for questioning. When the magistrates, John Hathorne and Jonathan Corwin, arrived, a huge crowd of spectators was milling around outside the tavern, so the authorities decided to move the proceedings to the village church, or meetinghouse, as it was called. In front of nearly the entire Salem Village community, Sarah Good was the first to be questioned.

The pregnant, disheveled, 38-year-old Good was already a person much disliked and distrusted in the community: she was a beggar in a society that believed poverty to be a sign of God's disfavor, she had a bad temper, and she had been known to utter what seemed like devilish curses under her breath when villagers refused to give her the food or tobacco for which she begged. (Indeed, it was not uncommon for New Englanders to tell their neighbors, in the midst of a dispute, to go to the devil.) Good was asked why she had not been coming to church regularly, and she replied that she did not own clothes decent enough to wear to service. Asked what she uttered to herself when she left a house, Good claimed she was saying her Psalms. But when questioned further, she was unable to remember the words to any Psalms. Good's case was not helped when her husband, with whom she had a bitter relationship, yelled out in the middle of the questioning that his wife was "an enemy to all good."

As Good vehemently denied the allegations against her, chaos broke out in the meetinghouse. The afflicted

girls, who had been calm and composed a moment earlier, now began wailing and crying out, accusing Sarah Good of tormenting them at that very moment. Still, Good refused to confess to witchcraft, suggesting that Sarah Osborne was really to blame.

The magistrates then turned their attention to Osborne. This sickly and aging woman was also somewhat of an outcast in the community, for she had not attended church in more than a year. Many years earlier, after her husband died, she had allowed a male servant to remain

This 1593 engraving depicts Native Americans being tormented by demons. A full century later, the Puritans believed that all Indians were in league with the Devil.

living in the house with her, and had later married him. Her choices in this matter were considered scandalous, so she had stopped attending services to avoid the stares and the gossip. At her examination, Osborne insisted she was innocent of the charges. Indeed, she argued that she was more likely to have been a victim of witchcraft than a practitioner. She spoke of a bad dream in which she had been pricked by a devilish apparition, "a thing like an Indian" (an allusion to the fact that Puritans believed all Indians to be in league with the Devil). Osborne also spoke of hearing voices in her head, urging her not to go to church. The magistrates interpreted these voices and the nightmare as evidence not of Osborne's bewitchment but of her guilty association with invisible specters.

Finally Tituba was called to the stand. Like the others, she at first denied the charges of witchcraft and said she didn't know why the children were suffering so. But Magistrate Hathorne was tenacious in his questions.

> "What is it that hurts them?" he asked.
> "The devil for ought I know," she replied.
> "How doeth he appear when he hurts them? With what shape? What is he like that hurts them?"
> "Like a man, I think."

Between one moment and the next, Tituba had gone from saying she knew nothing ("The devil for [all] I know") to conjecturing that this devil appears in the form of a man. Suddenly, the floodgates opened. Had Tituba stayed silent at this moment, or stuck to her denials, perhaps the whole witch episode would have quickly blown over. Witch-hunts had already fallen out of favor in Europe and were exceedingly rare in the colonies. Witchcraft proceedings in New England courts numbered in the few dozen over many decades, and in most cases, judges and juries found a lack of evidence supporting the accusations. Accused witches were generally let off with a warning not to dabble in devilry. Perhaps this would have been the case in Salem if Tituba had not taken the stand. For reasons that we may speculate on but never know entirely, Tituba chose another path.

"She confessed," biographer Elaine G. Breslaw wrote, "to consorting with the Devil, blaming Sarah Good and Sarah Osborne for forcing her to take part in a plot to hurt the children, and proceeded to elaborate on a fantastic chronicle describing a coven of witches in Boston [where she and the Parris family had once lived], suggesting with telling detail how satanic power had infiltrated their Salem community. The girls quieted as they listened with astonishment to her extraordinary story, an account of witchcraft so inspired and singular that it appeared to be plausible."

Tituba described the Devil as a tall man with black clothes and white hair, who could take the shape of a great black dog, or a hog, or black and red rats. (In her confession itself, this man was no doubt a white man, but later accounts of the story transformed him into a brown or black man, reflecting the Puritans' fears that Indians and Africans were likely to be the Devil's helpers.) She had met him in Boston and in the woods around Salem. He was seen suckling a yellow bird between his fingers— his devilish animal companion, usually called a "familiar." He carried a book that he urged Tituba to sign, promising to give her pretty things if she served him, or to harm her if she refused. She became a witch, she said, and saw many other witches flying around on sticks in the middle of the night. The witches, Tituba said, had transformed into specters—disembodied evil spirits—and had tried to kill some of the children, including Betty Hubbard and Ann Putnam.

Although some early historians accused Tituba of spouting incoherent nonsense (a reflection, perhaps, of

The slave of Puritan minister Samuel Parris, Tituba (shown here swooning during her testimony) played a pivotal role in the Salem episode. For reasons that are unknown, she confessed to consorting with the Devil and provided detailed descriptions of wide-spread satanic influence in the community.

racial prejudice), more recent interpreters argue that Tituba's tale was a carefully crafted story that provided exactly the answers the magistrates were looking for. We'll never know for sure: as a slave, Tituba had no way to record her own motives or thoughts at the time, and after the trials, she was sold to another master and disappeared from the historical record. But this utterly powerless woman's "fantastic chronicle" had a huge impact on later events, for it corroborated the afflicted girls' claims that they could see the "specters" that tormented them. This so-called spectral evidence would soon become the only proof necessary to send an accused witch to the gallows. Rarely had a slave ever held such influence over those who enslaved her.

With Tituba, Good, and Osborne manacled and shipped off to await trial in the Boston jail, the magistrates now renewed their questioning of the afflicted. From the pulpit of the meetinghouse, Samuel Parris spoke out vehemently against witchcraft and warned that Satan's minions might be found even among churchgoers. Around this time, Salem's former preacher, Deodat Lawson, returned to town and also fumed from the pulpit that the Evil One had indeed come to the village, and that he was not capable of taking the form of an innocent person. This was a key piece of preaching, and a controversial one. There were those in centuries and years past who argued the opposite: that it was indeed possible for the Devil to deceive by appearing in the spectral form of someone who was, in reality, a godly person. Lawson's assertion meant that all "visions" of witches—whether they appeared to the afflicted in daydreams or nightmares— served as evidence that the actual person was indeed one of Satan's servants.

Soon after the first questionings, 12-year-old Ann Putnam cried out the name Martha Corey in the midst of a fit, but her parents, Ann and Thomas, hushed her—for Corey was no slave or outcast, but a fine, upstanding member of the congregation. Despite Lawson's preaching, it was still difficult for Salem villagers to imagine that one of their best community members could be a witch. Corey had, however, publicly opposed the witchcraft proceedings and did not believe the girls were truly bewitched, so she was perhaps a natural target for their growing frenzy. Two weeks later, Abigail Williams stood up in the middle of a church service and cried, "Look where Goodwife Corey sits upon the beam suckling her yellow bird betwixt her fingers!" Young Ann Putnam immediately cried out that she was seeing the same spectral image. Despite Corey's high reputation, she was arrested the next day. Because she had heard all the gossip about her, Corey told the constable she'd been expecting his arrival. Later on, the magistrates took this comment as evidence that Corey was indeed a witch, who perhaps had the power to foresee the future.

By the time of Corey's interrogation on March 21, a middle-aged woman named Gertrude Pope had joined

(continued on page 40)

WHO WAS TITUBA?

Tituba, Samuel Parris's household slave, is one of the most widely recognized names associated with the Salem tragedy, yet her image remains clouded by mysteries and misconceptions. Some historians have charged her with instigating the entire tragedy by introducing West Indian magic to Betty Parris and Abigail Williams through fantastic stories from her homeland.

If Tituba was originally from Africa, as some historians believe, she would likely have been acquainted with various "white magic" ceremonies similar to this shamanic ritual dance from modern-day Nigeria.

Others note her pivotal early confession and the way its fanciful, vivid imagery determined the structure and content of all later confessions. Still others assign her a relatively passive role. To this day, scholars debate not only her role in the trials but her biography prior to her dramatic actions and confession in 1692. After 1693, when she was allowed by Parris to languish in jail until he could arrange to sell her to another master, there are no records of what happened to her.

No one knows for sure whether Tituba was of black African or Native American ethnicity, although it seems relatively clear that Parris purchased her while living at his father's plantation on the West Indian island of Barbados. Elaine Breslaw, author of a book-length study entitled *Tituba, Reluctant Witch of Salem,* believes that Tituba was an Arawak Indian. "Planters in Barbados favored women slaves in general and Amerindian women in particular," Breslaw argues, for the other available populations— Irish and African—were considered lazy and dangerous in comparison. She also notes that Arawaks were reputed to be very fond of children, an attribute that would have rendered Tituba ideal for domestic work in her master's eyes. But legal historian Peter Charles Hoffer, author of *The Devil's Disciples,* insists that Tituba is a Yoruba name and that she was therefore most likely a black African, possibly from the Gold Coast area, which is now known as Ghana. For a number of complex historical and cultural reasons, the possibility that Tituba was of mixed Indian/African heritage is considered unlikely by both Hoffer and Breslaw.

In the records, Tituba is always referred to as an Indian, and it seems unlikely that this reference is strictly a reflection of her marriage to a man who was almost definitely Native American, one John Indian. Tituba's racial background is such an important issue because it would have determined what kinds of magical practices she may have known about, and would have affected the way her Puritan masters envisioned her. Indians were closely associated with the Devil in Puritan theology, so it would have been easy for Parris to blame Tituba for bringing the witchcraft "contamination" into his household and community. If Tituba were actually an African, however, she may have been "transformed" into an Indian woman by trial commentators and later historians precisely because they still tended to associate Native Americans with witchcraft. Hoffer, who favors this approach, also argues that Tituba would certainly have known a little magic from her native Yoruban culture—relatively harmless practices she may have described to Betty and Abigail. Breslaw, in contrast, takes Tituba at her word. During her confession, she insisted that she had never done anything close to witchcraft before Mary Sibley arrived in the Parris household with the recipe for witch cake (an English folk-magical tradition).

The debates on these ideas will no doubt be examined by generations of scholars to come. But one fact seems relatively inarguable: for a brief, painful, and ultimately tragic moment, Tituba reversed the master-slave hierarchy of power in that meetinghouse 300 years ago. She made her confession, and in doing so, saved her own life. We will never know whether she did it consciously or instinctively—or whether she would have hesitated to speak if she understood that her confession would jeopardize the lives of other people.

(continued from page 37)
the ranks of the afflicted and was likewise suffering fits. (Pope was but the first of many adults, male and female, who eventually came forward with complaints of bewitchment and torment by the devilish "specters" of certain fellow villagers.) When Martha Corey was brought in front of the magistrates, a strange new symptom appeared in her accusers. As historian Lori Lee Wilson relates,

Whenever she bit her lip, the young women's teeth clamped down on their lips and they cried out in pain; whenever Martha folded her hands in front of her

[during what was probably an arthritis attack], the girls screamed that she pinched them, and the backs of their hands were visibly bruised. When Martha leaned against the chair in front of her, Gertrude Pope doubled over, complaining that the witch Corey was tearing her bowels out.

Martha Corey, convinced that these "symptoms" were fraudulent and that her accusers were afflicted with nothing more than a case of wicked theatrics, laughed out loud at their apparent sufferings. Her sarcastic attitude enraged the afflicted—Gertrude Pope even took off a shoe and hurled it at Corey, hitting her in the head—and encouraged the magistrates to send this insolent witch Corey to the Boston prison without further ado.

Unlike the first few women accused of witchcraft, Martha Corey, seen here at her trial, was a respected member of the community. Corey's failure to take seriously the girls' absurd accusations may have ultimately cost her life.

Betty Parris, who had been the first to suffer fits, was no longer among the accusers. Her parents packed her up and sent her off to her aunt and uncle's home in Salem Town. Betty, who continued to have fits there, told her relatives that the "great Man in Black" was still tormenting her, trying to recruit her as his servant and promising her "whatsoever she desired." Betty's aunt told the young girl that the next time Satan appeared to her, she should call him a liar and be done with him. Betty reportedly took her aunt's advice, and soon thereafter, the fits stopped as mysteriously as they had started.

Betty was gone, but the elder Ann Putnam was now among the accusers. A few weeks earlier, exhausted by the terrible symptoms suffered by both her daughter Ann and her maidservant Mercy Lewis, Mrs. Putnam lay down for a nap and was overcome by specters. In her sleep, she said, Martha Corey and Rebecca Nurse—an old churchly woman, also of high repute—had pressed down on her chest. Ann Putnam had recently lost a baby to illness, a six-week-old girl named Sarah, and was still grieving terribly. But if the magistrates had any doubts about her state of mind, they did not let that hinder them. When Ann claimed that the specter of a neighbor named John Willard had come to her to say he'd been responsible for Sarah's death, the witch-hunters believed her. Willard would be tried and executed later that year.

At the end of March, several more were "cried out" and then arrested—Rebecca Nurse and her equally pious sisters, Mary Easty and Sarah Cloyce, and four-year-old Dorcas (short for Dorothy) Good. In her tearful interrogation, little Dorcas held out her finger and showed the magistrates a deep red spot about the size of a flea bite, then told them it was the place where she had suckled her familiar, a little snake.

April saw the accusations, examinations, and imprisonments of 23 more suspected witches, including John

and Elizabeth Proctor, Bridget Bishop (who would be the
first to hang later that year), and Giles Corey (who would
be pressed to death). George Burroughs, Parris's predeces-
sor in the role of Salem Village preacher, was accused and
then hauled back from his new home in Maine. By the
end of May, the prisons in Salem and other neighboring
towns were full: nearly 100 people had been locked up and
no bail was granted. It was during this period that sickly
Sarah Osborne died while still in chains, and Dorcas Good
witnessed her shackled mother giving birth to a baby
sister who would not survive more than a few weeks.

In June, the colonial government established a special
court to hear the witch cases. According to the colonial governor, William Phips, the presiding judges were "persons of
the best prudence and figure that could then be pitched
[relied] upon." But none of these men had been trained as
lawyers, a fact that later historians would find quite significant. At the time, however, Phips had no reason to doubt
that these men would apply rationalism and solid Christian
principles to this direst of situations.

Evidence
Considered

An engraving depicting the first New World Sabbath service of the Pilgrims. The Puritans' fierce religiosity was directed toward—and supposedly demonstrated —the eternal salvation of their souls, but all-too-worldly jealousies and petty disputes inevitably crept into Puritan society.

3

The ancestors of the New England Puritans who became embroiled in the Salem witch hysteria were reformers who journeyed to the New World to escape religious intolerance in England. In the end, however, the Puritans found a large measure of intolerance among themselves.

In the mid-16th century, England had been ruled by King Henry VIII—a power-hungry, aggressive, often ruthless leader who married six times, fought numerous wars, and hugely expanded the scope of royal government during his nearly 40 years on the throne. Midway through his reign, Henry broke away from the Roman Catholic Church and the authority of the pope by establishing the Church of England.

Across Europe at this time, the Reformation was under way. Sparked

Henry VIII, who ruled Britain from 1509 to 1547, split with the Roman Catholic Church and created the Church of England. But Henry's refusal to eliminate all vestiges of Catholicism from the Anglican religion spurred the Puritans to establish their own sect.

by the protest writings of Martin Luther, many reform-minded Christians broke away from papal authority and established their own (Protestant) religions. The Puritans were a group of such reformers who vehemently rejected most Catholic traditions and wanted to "purify" the Church of England of all Catholic influence. When King Henry demonstrated an unwillingness to follow such an extreme path, the Puritans withdrew from the Church of England and founded their own religion.

Puritanism was a cohesive movement at the start, but

eventually it splintered into several groups, including Quakers and Separatists. Those who still went by the label "Puritan" adhered to a strict form of Calvinism, a religious philosophy asserting that all humans were born sinful, but—by eternal decree of God—some would be saved through Christ's righteousness. While no one could be certain whom God would elect for salvation, those who experienced a conversion experience (a sudden communion with the Holy Spirit) were considered good candidates. According to Puritan theology, a person could prepare for this conversion only through a life stressing self-discipline, introspection, and an avoidance of all sinfulness. Sin and wantonness were fairly broadly defined by Puritan custom and law, and included such things as dancing around the maypole (a popular pastime in England) or wearing bright clothing. Puritans were not averse to wealth—in fact, it was considered a sign of God's grace to be blessed with riches—but they forbade excessive displays of it. Puritans believed themselves to be God's chosen people, but to Anglicans (members of the Church of England) and other Christians, Puritans seemed self-righteous, bigoted, narrow-minded, and hypocritical—just as the adjective deriving from their name, "puritanical," still implies.

In 1629, after decades of suffering ridicule and intolerance in England, the Puritans requested and received a charter (a set of laws) from King Charles I giving them the right to settle and govern the English colony in Massachusetts Bay. In 1630, a lawyer named John Winthrop sailed with about 1,000 Puritan colonists for the New World, where they would establish a godly community—a beacon for righteousness in this wicked world, a spearhead of saintliness in the battle against the Devil. These were not merely metaphorical or literary ideas, but very literal and serious ones. "We must consider

"The eyes of all people are upon us," John Winthrop (center) told the Puritan colonists who sailed with him to Massachusetts Bay in 1630. "If we shall deal falsely with our God . . . and to cause him to withdraw his present help from us, . . . we shall open the mouths of enemies to speak evil of the ways of God."

that we shall be as a City upon a Hill, the eyes of all people are upon us," Winthrop told the colonists. "If we shall deal falsely with our God in this work we have undertaken and to cause him to withdraw his present help from us, we shall be made a story . . . through the world, we shall open the mouths of enemies to speak evil of the ways of God."

The first generations of Puritans suffered terrible hardships in New England: epidemic illnesses, harsh winters, crop failures, and vengeful attacks from displaced Native Americans, whom Puritans considered to be tawny-skinned agents of the Devil. Hardships like these might have brought communities closer to one another, but instead the stresses of such a life provided fertile ground for discontent and hostility. While publicly continuing to believe they were God's chosen people, individual Puritans must have secretly begun to doubt their "elected" status, judging from the terrible suffering they'd endured. The Puritans believed in salvation through God's grace, but they also believed they could lose God's favor if they failed to lead saintly lives.

By the time of the witch trials, most Puritan communities were rife with internal battles, often in the form of bitter, drawn-out land disputes fueled by gossip and greed. Court settlement of lawsuits rarely resulted in a happy ending, but instead added fuel to the fire and encouraged an endless chain of countersuits. A larger threat to the community's security resulted from the fact that, ever since Governor Andros was forced from office nearly a decade earlier, the Massachusetts colony had been operating without an official charter from England, leaving all private property claims in a questionable state. A new charter was put in place in 1688 and Governor William Phips installed at that time, but the uneasy situation had brought all sorts of tensions and hostilities to the surface.

There were numerous other "stress factors," as we would call them today. Through its colonial government England was engaged in ongoing wars with Frenchmen and Indians, and casualties from those conflicts were everywhere. Although recent laws forbade Puritans to persecute Quakers and other denominations that had also taken refuge on the colonial shores of America, intolerance, fear, and bigotry persisted. Perhaps rebelling against their fractious, infighting parents and reflecting the

A devout Puritan lectures wayward imbibers outside an inn. By the time of the Salem witch hysteria, church attendance was way down and many Puritans, particularly the young, seemed unwilling to reject all worldly pleasures.

community's overall unrest, the younger generation of Puritans engaged in behavior that shocked their elders: growing their hair longer than was the custom, drinking, loitering, and socializing in public with members of the opposite sex. Regular church attendance was seriously on the decline throughout the colony, causing ministers and common people alike to fear Satan's influence all the more. Into these troubled waters came the accusations of witchcraft.

■   ■   ■

Bridget Bishop, a woman in her late fifties, was the first Salem witch to be tried, though she was not among the first to be accused. Later historians have suggested that the court deliberately chose Bishop as the first to stand trial: chances were, she'd be found guilty.

She was not at all protected by a good reputation (as were Martha Corey or Rebecca Nurse, for example), had lived in isolation on the outskirts of the village, and had been decried as a witch on numerous occasions over the years. A shrewd businesswoman who ran a prosperous inn, Bishop had been widowed twice, was married to a third husband, and indulged in a taste for bright, colorful clothing that offended the sensibilities of her more traditional Puritan neighbors. On June 2, she arrived in court wearing a lace-trimmed scarlet bodice.

There were several pieces of "evidence" against her: the affidavits of two confessed witches, Deliverance Hobbs and Mary Warren, various complaints from Salem villagers who believed Bishop to be the cause of all manner of misfortunes they had suffered over the years, and the report of a jury of matrons who had examined Bishop's body and found an unnatural "excrescence of flesh," taken to be a teat on which a familiar could suckle.

As if all this weren't enough to predispose the court against her, Bishop faltered and contradicted herself on the stand. "I am innocent to a witch, I know not what a witch is," she insisted. John Hathorne—a merchant from Salem Town who was part of both the original interrogation team and the present committee of court judges—pounced on the apparent contradiction. "How do you know then that you are not a witch?" Unable to answer this question to the court's satisfaction, Bishop was found guilty and sentenced to die.

On June 10, Bridget Bishop was led to a place that would soon come to be called Gallows Hill, where she was hanged. Her conviction and execution, rather than stemming the tide of accusations, only spread the contagion further abroad. Men and women in the nearby jurisdictions of Andover, Beverly, Rowley, and Boston now stood accused of satanic crimes. In certain cases, some of the afflicted girls from Salem were brought around to the houses of complete strangers in these outlying towns. There the magistrates would wait for the girls to fall into their fits or to see the specter of suspected witches, thereby justifying arrest. In Andover, the use of the "touch test" came into prominence. The touch test was based upon a belief that a tormenting specter must, upon contact, return to its owner. So the accused person would be asked or forced to lay her hand upon the afflicted girl. If the fit stopped, the touch test was deemed proof that the accused was a witch. Several Andover women, accused and tested in this manner, broke down and confessed, but later repented for having "belied" themselves.

Meanwhile, back in Salem, the universally disliked Sarah Good was the second person to stand trial; along with witchcraft, she was accused of murdering the infant she had given birth to in prison. She was found guilty, as were Susannah Martin, Elizabeth How, Sarah Wilds, and Rebecca Nurse shortly thereafter. Nurse's beloved stature in the community almost helped free her. Thirty-nine friends of the old woman, including young Ann Putnam's aunt and uncle, signed a petition in defense of Rebecca Nurse's good character, and 11 people stood witness in her favor. The evidence against her being rather weak, the jury found her not guilty. Immediately upon that announcement, the afflicted girls started shrieking and wailing, claiming that Rebecca's specter was killing them.

Seeing this, Justice William Stoughton, who presided over the Court of Oyer and Terminer (Latin for "hear and determine"), reminded the jury to consider a statement Rebecca had made when she saw Elizabeth Hobbs and her daughter—two confessed witches—stand up and

Memorial to Rebecca Nurse, whose well-to-do family managed to save her remains from the common grave where authorities dumped the bodies of the four other women executed with her on July 19, 1692.

testify against her. "What, do these give Evidence against me now? They used to come among us." This, Stoughton suggested, was nothing if not an admission that Rebecca had belonged to the coven of witches. One juror asked Rebecca to explain what she had meant by the statement "They used to come among us," but the old woman, hard of hearing and overcome by sorrow, did not answer. The jury went out a second time and brought back a guilty verdict. After the fact, Rebecca Nurse sent a written explanation to the court, saying she had not heard the juror's question, and that her statement simply reflected the fact that Hobbs and her daughter were once among the accused and had been held in the same prison cell as Nurse. Rebecca received a temporary reprieve from

Governor Phips, but the girls clamored against her once again. The reprieve was rescinded, and Rebecca Nurse was hanged along with four other women on July 19.

Rebecca's well-connected family came secretly in the night to remove her body from the gallows and to give her a Christian burial, despite laws against doing this for a condemned person. The four other bodies were dumped without ceremony in a shallow grave behind the gallows.

■   ■   ■

The nature of evidence used in criminal trials is, to this day, a subject of ongoing controversy. Toward the end of the 20th century, for example, the use of DNA (genetic) analysis became a standard way to identify criminals who leave behind hair, skin cells, or other physical evidence. In certain cases, persons convicted of crimes using all the old, traditional forms of evidence—even those sitting on death row awaiting execution—have been released after DNA testing reveals that their genetic "fingerprint" doesn't match the physical clues left at the crime. Confessions and witness testimony are also subject to continual legal and philosophical battles, because confessions can be falsified or coerced, and witnesses for the prosecution are often indicted criminals who've been given an incentive—a reduced prison term, for example to testify against their former accomplices.

The nature of allowable evidence at the Salem trials, and its disastrous consequences, marked a major turning point in the history of American justice. By the rules of the charter, colonial courts were supposed to conform their proceedings to English law, but English law had not yet developed solid rules of evidence. Furthermore, the modern requirement to prove a defendant guilty "beyond a reasonable doubt"—a standard whose exact meaning and application is still debated today—would not become a widely used concept in American courts for another 100 years. The idea of measuring the truth through objective, empirical means was beginning to emerge in English jurisprudence (legal theory), but for the most part, trials were still conducted primarily on circumstantial evidence and hearsay (statements made out of court by someone who isn't present to testify under oath). "In general," notes one historian of early American law, "judges allowed into evidence a wide array of assertions, tales, surmises, and gossip."

This generalization held true at Salem, although the court councilors appointed by Phips took the standard to a new extreme by allowing so-called spectral evidence: a witness's claim that the accused person's "specter" was tormenting him or her. At Salem in 1692, such a claim was considered hard evidence, especially if it was corroborated by other admissible items, such as the discovery of the Devil's "mark" on the accused person's body (a small red circle, usually found somewhere near the genitals, which would not bleed when pricked by a pin), or positive results of the touch test. Also admissible as proof of witchcraft was a person's inability to say the Lord's Prayer without error.

By modern standards of law, these items of "evidence" are laughable. But it would be wrong to assume that all participants and observers of the Salem trials were equally satisfied that such evidence constituted proof of witchcraft, for there were skeptics and dissenters even back then. Witch trials had virtually disappeared throughout Europe, and among learned judges and lawyers, "opinion was divided, although leaning strongly against the possibility that witches could do what was attributed to them," according to a prominent historian. Even those who believed that witches did indeed exist— the majority of people, no doubt—sometimes found reason to criticize and question the methods used to identify witches. In England about 100 years before the Salem trials, a man named Reginald Scott had ridiculed most of the claims made by witch-hunters and the confessed witches, dismissing them as the imaginative fancies of poets and gossipy old folks. Matthew Hale, a respected English jurist of the 1650s and 1660s, had upheld the reliability of spectral evidence, but in the decades following, other leading legal practitioners had become very doubtful.

But while the tide of opinion was beginning to turn against spectral and other such flimsy-seeming evidence among legal authorities in England, church authorities in Puritan Massachusetts continued to rely upon the older traditions. One reason this may have been so was that, unlike later Americans, Puritans did not believe in erecting a wall to separate "church" from "state." Man's law and God's law were, in theory and in practice, one and the same. For instance, under Massachusetts criminal codes written in the 1640s, biblical offenses such as disobeying one's parents or blaspheming were considered capital crimes. Although it's not clear that anyone was actually executed for such violations, these laws sent a strong message to the community about staying within the boundaries of good, godly conduct as Puritan tradition defined it.

Arguably the most significant "keeper" of Puritan tradition at the time of the Salem ordeal was the Reverend Cotton Mather. The son of Increase Mather—the president of Harvard College and an extremely influential preacher—Cotton Mather believed deeply that Massachusetts was bedeviled by a growing legion of witches. These, he felt, had to be stopped at all costs, and so he argued strongly in favor of using spectral evidence, touch tests, and devil's marks. Other clergymen—most notably the

Reverend Samuel Willard of Boston—spoke out in great fear that innocent lives were threatened by the horribly inexact and potentially fraudulent methods of the witch-hunt. But Mather was a far more powerful figure in the colonial ministry than Willard, so the court at Salem followed his lead—at least in the beginning. Eventually, the tide would turn against him.

■   ■   ■

On August 5, 1692, a few weeks after the hanging of Rebecca Nurse, six more people were brought to trial and convicted of witchcraft. Among them was Martha Carrier, an Andover resident who'd been arrested in May while visiting relatives in Salem. Her four children had been imprisoned as well. Carrier's eldest sons, 15 and 17, were tortured—their heels were tied up around their necks—and eventually confessed that their mother was a witch and that they themselves had practiced witchcraft for one month. The younger Carrier children, a boy of 10 and a girl of 7, may have witnessed the torture of their brothers, for they too confessed. John Proctor and his pregnant wife, Elizabeth, also stood trial that August 5; their son had like-wise been tortured to obtain a denunciation of his parents. John Willard (a constable who had refused to arrest accused witches, and was soon after "cried out" himself), George Jacob Sr., and George Burroughs (a former Salem preacher, who'd been unpopular with his congregation) also came before the court that day. All were convicted and sentenced to hang two weeks later, although Elizabeth Proctor was granted a reprieve because she was three months pregnant.

Sanctioned by the church through Cotton Mather, and upheld by popular hysteria, fear, and vengeance, the well-oiled Salem witch-killing machine ran on. But there were already signs that the machinery would soon break down. Before his trial, John Proctor had written a terse but eloquent letter to Increase Mather, pointing out the court's illegal use of force and torture, and questioning its reliance on spectral evidence. This letter, among other testimony, would eventually move colonial authorities to shut down the Court of Oyer and Terminer. On August 19 at the gallows, the Reverend George Burroughs spoke out to defend his innocence, urging the judges to reconsider their methods. As he spoke, the afflicted girls and women pointed at him and said they saw the Devil dictating to him. Burroughs closed his speech with a perfect recitation of the Lord's Prayer—something that Satan allegedly prevented his followers from doing. Deeply moved by this counterevidence, the crowd of spectators pushed forward as if they might rescue Burroughs. Cotton Mather rode into the crowd on horseback and shouted out that they were being deceived. "The devil has often been transformed into an angel of light," he exclaimed. The hanging of Burroughs proceeded as planned. But it was here that many observers really began to wonder if they were witnessing the execution of innocents.

Still, the process continued. In early September, six more were tried and sentenced to death: Mary Easty, Alice Parker, Ann Pudeator, Dorcas Hoar, Mary Bradbury, and Martha Corey, the cantankerous, sarcastic, proud old woman who'd laughed at the afflicted girls' torments. Giles Corey, Martha's 80-year-old husband, had also been accused but refused to testify. Corey had watched his wife and the others be convicted and hanged one by one; he undoubtedly realized he was facing the same fate. By standing mute, he refused to acknowledge the authority of the court. So the court, by law, could not try him for the alleged crimes. Their process stalled, the judges ordered Corey to be tortured. Jailers laid him on his

Eighty-year-old Giles Corey (seen here at his trial) refused to answer the charges leveled against him. Authorities ultimately "pressed" Corey to death in an unsuccessful attempt to extract a confession.

back, placed a board over him, and stacked large rocks on top of the board one by one. At one point, when the tip of Corey's tongue was being forced out between his teeth, someone unceremoniously poked it back into his mouth. If they had been hoping to get a confession from the old man, they failed: his ribs were crushed and he died without speaking a word.

Corey's refusal to speak wasn't the only rebellious message he sent to the court. Days before his death, he transferred all his property to two of his sons-in-law. Salem magistrates had grown all too accustomed to confiscating the land and homes of executed witches, but now they couldn't touch Corey's assets. It was a relatively small gesture, for it didn't save his life. But for a moment, a proud old man's foresight had stopped the court in its bloody, greedy tracks.

Believers
and Skeptics

Sometimes the mere presence of a mole or wart doomed a suspected witch. The Puritans considered such a growth on the skin evidence that the accused was suckling a "familiar," a demonic companion that took the form of an animal.

4

By September, the jails of Salem, Andover, Boston, Ipswich, and other nearby towns were packed with more than 200 accused witches. The eight people hanged on September 22—Martha Corey, Mary Easty, Alice Parker, Mary Parker, Ann Pudeator, Margaret Scott, Wilmot Redd, and Samuel Wardwell—would turn out to be the last casualties of the trials, but the accusations and arrests had not yet stopped. Betty Parris was hidden away at the home of her uncle, Samuel Sewall, on Main Street in Salem Town, just around the corner from the two-story courthouse where the trials were taking place. But the other accusers—the so-called afflicted "girls," whose ranks now included several mature women as well as a few men, such as Tituba's husband, John Indian—continued to cry out the names of specters allegedly tormenting them. They had started at the bottom of the communal ladder with the shunned, impoverished Sarah Good and had generally stuck to naming persons of relatively low social status, with a few notable exceptions such as Rebecca Nurse and her sisters. The proceedings of the Court of Oyer and Terminer reflected this same kind of class bias, whether intentionally or not: Of the 19 defendants brought to trial almost immediately, almost all had low social status in their communities. Higher-status suspects were not brought to trial immediately, and in that extra space of time, several well-to-do prisoners mustered the resources and found the opportunity to escape.

But the accusations themselves had already spread beyond the relatively powerless. When one girl cried out against the Reverend Samuel Willard—a highly respected Boston clergyman who'd been speaking out against the court since early summer—even Justice Stoughton paused from the vigorous pace of convictions and executions. He quashed the accusation and ordered the accuser out of the courtroom. (Willard tried to publish his suspicions that the girls were untruthful in their accusations, but he was banned from doing so by Governor Phips's "gag proclamation" aimed at silencing the opposition.) Later, the accusers would dare to point the finger at the wives of the most powerful politician in the colony, Governor Phips himself, and the most influential theocrat, Increase Mather.

By late summer and early fall, the voices of dissent had grown quite forceful. George Burroughs's eloquent speech, given just moments before his hanging, illuminated an undercurrent of opposition to the way the trials were proceeding. Dissent came, of course, from defendants themselves, although not always as a last-ditch attempt at self-preservation: Mary Easty, for example, addressed her eloquent plea to Justice Stoughton and the other judges, saying she was prepared to die herself, but begging the court to consider the "wiles and subtlety of my accusers"

A 1790 woodcut showing the Salem courthouse, where, a century before, the accused witches had been tried.

and to "examine these afflicted persons strictly" to avoid the shedding of more innocent blood.

Meanwhile, 50 or more confessed witches were now languishing in prisons across the county, awaiting the court's decision as to a fitting punishment. Remarkably, not a single confessed witch had been put to death, but 19 defendants who had all insisted on their innocence were now dead. This pattern reversed the age-old tradition by which even confessed witches, no matter how remorseful and penitent, would have to be put to death. God demanded nothing less, it was believed. In Salem, although it had become obvious that confession was a sure way to spare one's life, many of those who'd confessed now came forward to recant. A particularly moving recantation came from several women of Andover: Mary Osgood, Mary

Tiler, Deliverance Dane, Abigail Barker, Sarah Wilson, and Hannah Tiler. In a paper filed with the Court of Oyer and Terminer, they described how they'd been completely overwhelmed by their accusers, as well as by the "gentlemen" in charge of the process—in other words, the magistrates and jailers:

> [W]e were blindfolded, and our hands were laid upon the afflicted persons, they being in their fits, and falling into their fits at our coming into their presence (as they said) and some led us and laid our hands upon them, and then they said they were well, and that we were guilty of afflicting of them; whereupon we were all seized as prisoners . . . and forthwith carried to Salem. And by reason of that sudden [surprise], we knowing ourselves altogether innocent of that crime, we were all exceedingly astonished and amazed, and consternated and affrighted even out of our reason; and our nearest and dearest relations, seeing us in that dreadful condition, and knowing our great danger, apprehending that there was no other way to save our lives . . . but by confessing ourselves to be such and such persons as the afflicted represented us to be. . . .
>
> And indeed that confession, that is said we made, was no other than what was suggested to us by some gentlemen; they telling us, that we were witches, and they knew it, and we knew it, and they knew that we knew it, which made us think that it was so; and our understanding, our reason, and our faculties almost gone, we . . . said anything and everything which they desired.

But those whose lives were not obviously endangered began to speak out as well. Indeed, after the very first trial on June 2, one of the appointed judges, Nathan Saltonstall—a farmer and soldier from nearby Haverhill, a frequent appointee to various councils and courts, and a man considered to be fair and lenient in his judicial duties—resigned his

Samuel Sewall—the uncle of Betty Parris, one of the original afflicted girls—served as a judge during the Salem trials. Sewall's stature in the community enabled him to quash accusations against his friend Nathan Saltonstall.

seat in protest over the use of spectral evidence, torture, and coerced confessions. Soon after, the afflicted girls accused him of witchcraft, but his friend Samuel Sewall—also an appointee to the special Salem court—told them they were mistaken, and that was the end of that. (Sewall happened to be Betty Parris's uncle, with whom the young girl was now housed. Like his friend Saltonstall, Sewall also harbored doubts about the proceedings he participated in, but he chose not to speak out, making a public confession of his error only five years later.)

Thomas Brattle, age 32, was a wealthy Boston merchant, a distinguished mathematician and astronomer, and a treasurer of Harvard College. After witnessing a portion of the trials in the fall, Brattle penned a long, detailed, and trenchantly argued "open letter" that was circulated privately and eventually published. While carefully offering his respect to the governor and the appointed judges— "I would sooner bite my fingers' ends than willingly cast dirt on authority," he disclaimed at the start—Brattle, trained to believe in the dispassionate objectivity and logical analysis of the scientific method, did not hesitate to criticize the proceedings. "I never thought judges infallible; but reckoned that they, as well as private men, might err; and that when they were guilty of erring, standers by, who possibly had not half their judgment, might, notwithstanding, be able to detect and behold their errors."

Brattle first condemned the touch test. "I am fully persuaded that it is sorcery, and a superstitious method, and that which we have no rule for, either from reason or religion." He went on to reveal the (literally) devilish illogic of allowing confessed witches to testify against other accused persons:

> These confessors, (as they are called,) do very often contradict themselves, as inconsistently as is usual for any crazed, distempered person to do. This the Salem gentlemen do see and take notice of; and even the judges themselves have, at some times, taken these confessors in flat lies, or contradictions, even in the courts . . . but [instead of discarding such questionable testimony] the judges vindicate these confessors, and salve their contradictions, by proclaiming, that the devil takes away their memory, and imposes upon their brain. . . .
>
> But now, if, in the judges' account, these confessors are under the influence of the devil . . . why then should these judges, or any other men, [take] the words of these confessors, as [seriously as] they do?

Brattle also ridiculed the notion that discovering a "preternatural excrescence" (such as a mole, wart, or other "teat" for a familiar) should be proof positive of witchcraft. "I wonder what person there is, whether man or woman, of whom it cannot be said but that, in some part of their body or other, there is a preternatural excrescence." He called "silly and foolish" the argument that a prisoner who didn't shed tears in court (such as Martha Corey) should be assumed remorseless and guilty. "Some there are who never shed tears; others there are that ordinarily shed tears upon light occasions, and yet for their lives cannot shed a tear when the deepest sorrow is upon their hearts; and who is there that knows not these things?"

Finally, Brattle voiced his utter disbelief in spectral evidence. "These afflicted persons do say, and often have declared it, that they can see specters when their eyes are shut, as well as when they are open. . . . Can they see specters when their eyes are shut? I am sure they lie, at least speak falsely, if they say so; for the thing, in nature, is an utter impossibility." The "blind, nonsensical girls" might be imagining their tormentors while their eyes are shut, Brattle allowed, but this is not the same as "seeing" specters.

Brattle concluded his powerful letter with dire predictions about the impact these trials would have on the community and on future generations. "[I]f our officers and courts have apprehended, imprisoned, condemned, and executed our guiltless neighbors, certainly our error is great, and we shall rue it in the conclusion [regret it in the end]. . . . What will be the [result] of these troubles, God only knows; I am afraid that ages will not wear off that reproach and those stains which these things will leave behind them upon our land."

Brattle's voice reaches out across the centuries and appeals to modern ears; his logic and observational acumen were, by today's standards, impeccable. But Brattle was merely an observer, and neither a politician nor a clergyman. Worse yet, he was a merchant, a representative of the new individualist philosophy that seemed to threaten the Puritan values of community and faith. It would take a change of heart from within the Puritan theocracy itself before the witch-hunting factory was shut down.

Cotton Mather had been the de facto religious authority presiding over the trials, even though he didn't actually attend the proceedings. Four years earlier he had published a book entitled *Memorable Providences, Relating to Witchcrafts and Possessions,* in which he narrated cautionary tales of devilish doings throughout history. Mather's treatise was in some ways an extension of the work done by his father, Increase Mather, in the 1684 publication known as *Remarkable Providences.* These two books served as bridges between common folk-wisdom and the learned culture of highly educated clergy. As such, they reinforced and legitimized popular prejudices and fears about witches.

The elder Mather was one of New England's leading politicians and ministers. At the time he wrote his book, he believed that God was punishing the colonists for their declining piety through such terrors as King Philip's War with the Indians in 1675 and a series of smallpox epidemics. *Remarkable Providences* was written and distributed to the population to help bolster belief in the supernatural world and in Satan's doings, thereby inspiring common people to take the church and their commitment to God more seriously. In a very sober, reportorial tone, Increase Mather related stories of haunted houses, random objects flying telekinetically through the air, and—most notably—young women suffering demonic fits and speaking in tongues.

Though their society was highly literate, the Puritans lacked for anything that we might consider popular literature or books meant solely for entertainment. So a publication like *Remarkable Providences* would have been read by nearly every colonist, young and old. The same was true for the younger Mather's *Memorable Providences,* published

just five years later. Cotton, who was 30 years old at the time of the Salem crisis, had spent his entire life in the shadow of his illustrious and powerful father, and was often inspired to provide follow-ups and extensions to the elder man's work. But Cotton had a very different temperament; he was prone to emotional extremism and hysteria. His widely read book certainly played a catalytic role in the ensuing witch frenzy. (Indeed, *Memorable Providences* told the story of the Goodwin family of England, whose young girls began suffering mysterious body contortions and screaming fits in 1664. Betty Parris, Abigail Williams, and the other girls would almost certainly have read about the Goodwin children, and later historians would take this to mean that the afflictions of the Salem girls were the product of either human suggestibility or outright fraud.)

At the beginning of the troubles in Salem, Increase and Cotton Mather were equally concerned that the

Some Puritans viewed bloody conflicts with the Indians as a sign of God's displeasure at the settlers' impiety.

witches be rooted out quickly and that the Devil be chased from the community of God's chosen people. Now, as doubts about the proceedings mounted, father and son would part company.

We should understand that the "doubters" were not atheists, agnostics, or men who scoffed at the idea of the Devil's interference in human affairs. Instead, they were men of deep belief who had come to view the witch trials themselves as a form of communal bedevilment. Historian Peter Charles Hoffer puts it as follows:

> While Cotton was battling the Devil at arm's length, hurling sermons against the squadrons of specters which circled Salem, the Ministerial Association [the governing body of the Puritan religion, led by Increase Mather] was in more or less continuous session. Unlike Cotton, many of its members had traveled to Salem to see the first trials as well as the executions. Their advice . . . against the use of spectral evidence had been misunderstood (that was charitable) or ignored. Either way, they were not heard, and that rankled. To a man, they believed that the Devil was abroad, for his works were plain to see, and the trials must be his doing as well.

Samuel Willard had secretly published his dissent through a printer in Philadelphia, but Increase Mather—a man of conscience yet also a masterful politician—did not voice his doubts right away. For weeks he stayed on the sidelines and observed. He didn't want to offend, alienate, or do anything to weaken the administration of Governor Phips, whose appointment he had supported strongly. It had become clear that this spiritual, communal crisis was quickly becoming a political disaster as well. If Phips proved incapable of solving the witch problem, it would displease the English king and might cost Phips his job. So Increase Mather waited until the trials were suspended at the end of the summer, then came out with a treatise entitled *Cases of Conscience,* which he presented to the Ministerial Association on October 3. In it, he described the retractions by the Andover women and warned against the danger of accusing innocent people, especially those with good, churchgoing reputations. It would be better, he said, "that ten suspected Witches should escape than that one innocent Person should be condemned."

Willard was delighted; Cotton Mather was not. He immediately began to compile his brimstone-and-hellfire summer sermons into a publication that would rebut his father's book.

Meanwhile, Governor Phips—who had just returned from the war front—understood the implications of Increase Mather's text, and immediately halted the use of spectral evidence. Justice Stoughton was outraged and quit the bench. Phips wrote to the court authorities in London saying that he now "found that the Devill had taken upon him the name and shape of severall people who were doubtless innocent." On October 29, Phips dissolved the Court of Oyer and Terminer.

In November, colonial authorities established yet another court to try the remaining prisoners. Spectral evidence was strictly forbidden. By the spring, jurors acquitted 49 of the 52 remaining prisoners, while the 3 found guilty were pardoned. In May, Phips emptied the jails and sent prisoners home—although some, such as Tituba, still languished there, unable to pay the required fees for food and upkeep during their imprisonment. Soon enough, prisoners, their relatives, and relatives of executed witches approached the court authorities to obtain reparations. This round of petitions dragged on for decades afterward. The General Court ultimately repudiated the trials and began the fractious process of paying out claims. The children of George Burroughs were still filing papers for reparations

Spurred by the growing skepticism of the prominent Puritan minister Increase Mather, Governor William Phips (pictured here) banned the use of so-called spectral evidence in the witchcraft trials. Ultimately Phips dissolved the court hearing the accused witches' cases.

with the legal authorities 50 years later.

Increase Mather's powerful and thoughtful *Cases of Conscience* helped end the trials, but it also reverberated far beyond Salem in late 1692, for it turned out to be "what amounts to the first American tract on evidence" and "simply one of the great works of American legal literature," according to Hoffer. *Cases* began with the idea that the more horrible the crime, the more cautious we should be in our accusations and prosecutions of suspects. (This was an idea voiced earlier by Samuel Willard.) Mather then laid out certain principles that would become the forerunners of two crucial concepts in modern law, "probable cause" and "reasonable doubt."

His words also echoed a concept that had not yet become enshrined in Western law: the presumption of innocence.

Mather cautioned juries to be "charitable" as long as the accused person's innocence had the most evidence in its favor. If the testimony and other evidence "do not infallibly prove the crime against the person accused, [the court] ought not to determine him guilty of it." He further went on to discuss the problem of confessions tainted by the coercion of authorities or the derangement of the confessor.

Over the centuries and continuing through the present day, such legal ideas have been tested, refined, and revised again and again. We now shy away from the concept of "infallible proof," but we do attempt to define a standard of "reasonable doubt," which means there's enough ambiguity in the evidence to keep a reasonable, rational, average person from feeling certain about a defendant's guilt. "However criminal court judges charge the jury about the meaning of reasonable doubt, the jurors are to reach their conclusions through their reasoning powers, not their moral sense," explains legal historian Peter Charles Hoffer. In other words, mere beliefs, prejudices, or fears are not enough to accuse or convict a person of a serious crime.

Even at the dawn of the 21st century, with DNA testing, advanced ballistic analysis, and all sorts of scientific tools at our disposal, we know that criminal law is not and will never be an exact science. Beliefs, prejudices, and fears are only human and will always play a part in our attempt to identify and punish wrongdoers. Only in rare cases can the "entire truth" be known about crimes that happen beyond the eyesight of significant numbers of witnesses—and even in those cases, it's clear that witnesses often mistake what they see, or misremember, or find reason to lie. And, as will be explained in later chapters, the problem of coerced or "deranged" or otherwise unreliable confessions continues to plague us— sometimes even in the context of modern-day "witchcraft."

Increase Mather, one of the most important thinkers in colonial New England, helped lay the foundations for such crucial American legal concepts as probable cause, reasonable doubt, and the presumption of innocence.

But to the extent that our legal system actually works—to the extent that it is at all capable, under the right circumstances, of separating the guilty from the innocent—we owe at least some portion of gratitude to a Puritan minister who died in 1723.

In the years following the witch trials, that minister's son, Cotton Mather, found himself amidst the recriminations and inquiries into what had gone wrong. It was he who had, in many ways, whipped up the witch frenzy; and he continued to believe in the rampant presence of Satan's minions in Salem, even after the tide of public opinion had started to turn in another direction. He published his argumentative response to his father in a 1693 book entitled *Wonders of the Invisible World,* then followed that up the next year with *A Brand Pluck'd Out of the Burning,* another collection of horrifying witch narratives. He told, for example, the story of young Mercy Short, a woman who had survived an Indian raid in Salmon Falls, New Hampshire, two years before the witch trials. Her entire family was slain, but she was captured and then ransomed back by Governor Phips's soldiers. In Boston, she was a servant in the jails when she went by Sarah Good's cell. Good asked her for tobacco, and when Mercy refused, she was immediately overtaken by fits, as Peter Charles Hoffer relates:

> The convulsions supposedly caused by the witch led to bouts of delirium, in which Short had complete recall of the Indian raid. She saw the Devil, who was at first black but later became tawny [like an Indian]. . . . The Devil and his minions bewitched, then tortured, then starved Short. Those who prayed with her and kept vigil saw her pain and heard her shrieking. She carried on monologues with the Devil and plainly feared that she would suffer the same fate as the condemned witches, for she named some of them. Then, overcome with her own emotions, she would "frolick" about and make fun of the ministers who came to save her. In these states, she could see specters, proof to Mather that his views had been correct all along.

Explanations,
Then and Now

Gallows Hill, also known as Witch Hill. It was here that 20 victims of the Salem witch-hunt were executed.

5

Satan was apparently still abroad in Massachusetts; he had simply taken a different form than the one most Puritans had been expecting. They had feared witches, but the true enemy had turned out to be the accusation and trial process itself, which had caused the death of innocent people. In the aftermath of the trials, specters were no longer the greatest tormentors of Salem's people—that task was accomplished all too well by their own guilty consciences. Although a few contemporary commentators and historians were bold enough to blame plain-old human ignorance, fear, and hysteria for the tragedy, many others felt that the witch trials had been the work of the Devil himself. Three years after the trials were ended, the colonial government set aside January 14 as a day of prayer, fasting, and abstinence from work, "so that all God's people may offer up fervent supplications unto him." The bloody territorial wars with Frenchmen and Indians had continued, several harvests had failed, diseases continued to ravage the population—and the government's official word was that all these things were the "manifold judgments" of an angry God. The official proclamation referred to the witch trials merely as the "late tragedy, raised among us by Satan and his instruments."

Shortly thereafter, the 12 jurors for the trials wrote a public statement begging forgiveness from their fellow citizens and from God, but likewise blaming the Evil One for their transgressions:

> We confess that we our selves were not capable to understand, nor able to withstand the mysterious delusions of the powers of darkness, and prince of the air; but were for want of knowledge in ourselves, and better information from others . . . we fear we have been instrumental with others, though ignorantly and unwittingly, to bring upon ourselves, and this people of the Lord, the guilt of innocent blood.

Such people—today we might call them the "survivors"—were clearly conflicted about their role in the tragedy: they simultaneously acknowledged their mistakes, yet offered excuses in the form of "mysterious delusions" or satanic interference. No doubt, they were utterly bewildered by their own actions. Most of them probably believed themselves to be good, righteous, loving, and compassionate persons—and under normal circumstances, most of them probably were. Later historians would gain the perspective and the analytical concepts to begin to explain how "good people" can be convinced to do very bad things without the help of supernatural evil forces.

Unlike his father, Cotton Mather remained convinced that the men and women executed as witches had indeed been doing the Devil's bidding, and he defended the process by which those people had been condemned.

Cotton Mather was still a leading authority figure in Puritan society, and although tainted by the trials, he would remain a powerful and influential man (unlike the Reverend Samuel Parris, who handled the aftermath of the trials very badly and was eventually forced to leave Salem). But a perspective opposing Mather's view was already germinating. As evidenced by Thomas Brattle's bold and eloquent letter, there were some men among the merchant class whose worldview reflected a new rationalist, scientific streak. These men—products of the so-called Enlightenment—had read and absorbed the rationalist philosophies of such writers as John Locke (1634–1704), René Descartes (1596–1650), and Baruch Spinoza (1632–1677). They believed themselves to be anti-superstitious without being anti-religious, "modern" but reverential, logical but pious.

Among this new set was Brattle's friend, a prosperous fellow businessman from Boston named Robert Calef. Calef had not witnessed the trials himself, but he spent several years compiling first-hand accounts, letters, and public documents in, essentially, the 17th-century equivalent of investigative journalism. Calef was not, however, a perfectly objective observer, for he had an ax to grind. Before finalizing his manuscript, Calef had wanted to sit down and discuss the tragic events with Mather. Mather, proud son of an educational and theocratic elite, had snubbed Calef, mocking him as an uneducated man, a blockhead, a "mere weaver who styled himself a merchant," historian Peter Charles Hoffer reports. Calef, in return, "pilloried Mather, who for all his books believed that devils walked the streets, clanking chains, stinking of brimstone." What good was all that book learning, Calef wondered, if it overwhelmed common sense? Hoffer has described both the impact and the limitations of Calef's perspective:

> With a stroke Calef inverted the superiority claimed by the ministers and elevated the natural skepticism of ordinary men of affairs. He [however] conveniently ignored the fact that popular clamor and popular fears had led to the crisis in the first place, for he believed that the crisis was the work of a conspiracy of ministers and magistrates.

No printer in New England would accept Calef's manuscript, the ironically titled *More Wonders of the*

Invisible World, seeing it as a libel against Cotton Mather. So Calef arranged for a London printer to publish the book and ship copies back to New England for sale. Although driven in large part by Calef's animosity toward Mather, *More Wonders* became the template for later historical accounts, especially those focusing on possible fraud and conspiracy. The first two sections of the book were a direct attack upon Mather's methods for identifying witches and curing the torments of those afflicted by witchcraft—methods Calef denounced as nonsense designed to hoodwink gullible people. The third section was a compilation of letters and petitions written by Salem's people, including complaints written by Rebecca Nurse's family demanding a public apology from Samuel Parris (a request he finally obliged in late 1694). The fourth section consisted of an exchange of letters between a Scottish ship chaplain, who argued in favor of prosecuting witches, and Calef, who dismissed the practice as superstitious and un-Christian.

The fifth section of *More Wonders* was the real meat of the book: a collection of accounts that suggested fraud and foul play on the part of the afflicted girls—"wenches who played their juggling tricks," as one observer bitterly put it—and their supporters. Calef pointed out that, after her frightful confession in court, Tituba claimed that her master, Samuel Parris, "did beat her and [otherwise] abuse her, to make her confess and accuse (such as he called) her sister witches." Among many events that smacked of mischief, Calef described one that took place during Sarah Good's trial. One of the afflicted girls cried out that Good was stabbing her, and held up a piece of a blade that was embedded in her clothing. Immediately, however, a young man who was watching the trial held up a knife that he'd accidentally broken the day before, in that very courtroom.

The shard fit the broken knife perfectly, and Justice Stoughton lightly chastised the girl for lying. But he did not throw her out of the courtroom or bar her from continuing her accusations, nor did he allow the clear proof of this fraud to cast doubt on any of the other proceedings. An allegedly "afflicted" girl had been caught in a blatant lie, coldly calculated and superbly performed in order to discredit another human being, but the process churned on as if nothing had happened.

The incident points to one of the central questions of the entire Salem witchcraft saga: What exactly was happening with these afflicted girls? Were they genuinely possessed? Were they faking? Were they unconsciously rebelling against their parents' strict Puritan culture? Were they engulfed by some kind of collective hysteria, not unlike the screaming euphoria that engulfs a crowd of modern teenage girls at a concert by a pop star?

These are questions that have never been, and will probably never be, answered conclusively. Many people have offered explanations, and there may be elements of truth in many such accounts. There have always been those who feel the whole thing was a fraud concocted by bored, overly imaginative girls and taken too seriously by their Devil-fearing parents. Some psychologically oriented observers have proposed that the original two sufferers, Betty Parris and Abigail Williams, were profoundly wracked by guilt at having disobeyed Reverend Parris—for they had dabbled in fortune-telling, which was considered a close cousin to outright sorcery. Their all-consuming guilt soon manifested itself as a psychosomatic illness (meaning their mental states had caused physical symptoms), which then turned into a mass hysteria as more of their young female friends succumbed to guilt and fear. It has also been proposed that the first two girls suffered genuine ailments that were

Could grain like this have caused the Salem witch hysteria? In 1976, a scientist examined the hypothesis that the Puritans had ingested rye infected with the ergot fungus, which causes hallucinations as well as seizures.

then copied by other young women, especially those who wanted to share in all the attention Betty and Abigail were receiving.

Historians of a more naturalist temperament have suggested that the girls had been eating hallucinogenic wild mushrooms, or that the rye bread in Salem was infected with a fungus called ergot, which can cause convulsions and seizures. The ergot theory was examined closely in 1976 by a scientist named Linnda R. Caporael, and many people still find it a persuasive hypothesis.

But as early as the mid-18th century, a historian named Thomas Hutchinson wrote that "there are a great number of persons who are willing to suppose the accusers to have been under bodily disorders which affected their imaginations." He was not overly impressed by such an explanation, saying that it was "kind and charitable, but seems to be winking the truth out of sight."

Still others have taken a sociological, quasi-feminist stance, emphasizing that Puritan girls lived under painfully strict rules, were expected to do chores, prepare themselves for marriage, and avoid idle fun—and there-fore had few outlets for their natural energy and imagi-nation. Under this interpretation, such "symptoms" as cursing, screeching, flailing one's limbs, or throwing Bibles were simply forms of "acting out"—a violent, possibly unconscious, and ultimately out-of-control rebellion by high-spirited girls against the godly culture that confined them.

Whatever motivated the girls in the first place, it seems clear (at least in retrospect) that many of the adults in Salem were driven to participate in the trials by factors other than a simple fear of witchcraft. It was Calef who first pointed out the central culpability of the Reverend Samuel Parris, and later historians have followed his lead. Parris was the London-born son of a prosperous plantation owner, who'd started his divinity studies at Harvard but never completed his degree. Before arriving in New England, Parris had tried, and mostly failed, to become a successful businessman in his father's mold: he had gone to Barbados to oversee the family plantation (this is where he would have purchased the slave Tituba), and had later moved to

Boston. Wherever he went, his business dealings invariably landed him in the middle of bitter lawsuits and unpaid debts. Late in life he apparently felt called to the ministry, but some modern historians have questioned his motives.

At the time, church authorities in Boston were engaged in a rancorous battle. Some, such as Increase Mather, fought to retain uniformity in worship and belief over all New England churches. Other reform-minded ministers wanted to allow diversity in religious practice. (The reformers would ultimately win, as we can see today from the seemingly infinite array of religious institutions that find a home here in this country.) "It was thus far more likely that Parris heard the quarreling of ministers than the voice of God, even though Puritans believed that their covenant was with the Lord," Peter Charles Hoffer has speculated. Parris, Hoffer believes, was drawn to the cloth more by the lure of controversy than by dreams of creating his own compassionate ministry.

Hoffer is relatively gentle on Parris, viewing him as a misguided, well-meaning zealot who could never quite make a place for himself in the world. Frances Hill, author of several well-known books about the Salem trials, takes a more cynical approach, seeing Parris as an exceedingly greedy, insensitive man. Indeed, in his actions after the trials—particularly his continual chastisement of Rebecca Nurse's surviving relatives for no longer attending church meetings—he certainly revealed a depth of stubbornness and callousness.

Whether a true villain or merely a very flawed human being, Parris was no doubt an outsider in Salem, "without," according to Hoffer, "the network of kin and long-term friends which can sustain a person in times of trouble." Upon his arrival, Parris embarked on difficult negotiations with the village citizens, demanding to be supplied with firewood and other forms of in-kind payment in addition to his salary, and most significantly, expecting to be given the deed to the parsonage house, which had always been considered public, communal property. Samuel Parris, although disliked by many of his congregants, had some very strong supporters: members of the Putnam family, especially Thomas Putnam, whose wife, Ann, and daughter Ann would eventually play critical roles in the unfolding witch drama.

Arriving in Salem village in 1689, Parris had unwittingly walked into the midst of a social and political mine field. Although it lay a good five miles down the road from Salem Town, Salem Village was considered an annex of its larger, more urban neighbor. Its residents were expected to attend services in the town meeting hall and to participate in the town's civic and religious life. But a conflict had long been brewing between the traditional farm culture of the Village and the new merchant culture of the Town (reflecting the larger such battle throughout the colonies). Salem Town, Hoffer explains, "was not much different from Boston—a port of entry into the hinterland for the products of the world, a place of debarkation for the produce of woods, fields, and gardens of New England." In short, it was an early capitalist marketplace, one that would eventually generate values very different from traditional Puritan ones: individualism and self-reliance as opposed to community cohesion. Salem Village, in contrast, was still predominantly rural and communal. Many of its residents feared that mercantile values would destroy the Puritan way of life. In 1663, one of Salem's first settlers warned his neighbors, "My fathers and brethren, this is never to be forgotten, that New England is originally a plantation of religion, not a plantation of trade."

As the historians Paul Boyer and Stephen Nissenbaum explained in their groundbreaking 1974 book, *Salem Possessed: The Social Origins of Witchcraft,* traditional Puritans viewed themselves as almost literally belonging to "one body," a singular, indivisible community that could not logically or practically allow for individual members to pursue "private" interests and goals. "For a person to pursue such a self-determined course," historian Frances Hill has written, "was as destructive and, ultimately, as absurd as for one part of the human body to pursue its own good: for a hand to refuse to release to the mouth the food it held in its grasp, for example, or for the mouth to refuse to pass along that food to the stomach." A Puritan had been raised from infancy to distrust his or her private will, which was considered the original sin that got Adam and Eve ousted from Eden. "It was this innate self-interest—more than sexual lust, more than any of the 'sins' we commonly (and mistakenly) think of as particularly repugnant to the Puritans—that had to be tamed if it could not be eradicated," Hill explains. Yet self-interest was (and remains today) the driving engine of the new capitalist philosophy.

The Putnams were traditional villagers who yearned to be cut loose from the disturbing mercantilist developments in Salem Town—an independence that could only truly take place if the Village were allowed to establish a church of its own, thereby severing it from the Town's civic institutions. The Putnams were therefore desperate to see the newly arrived minister, Parris, ordained. The separation and ordination were eventually granted, but they had been opposed bitterly by another powerful clan in the Village, the Porters. Rebecca Nurse, it turns out, was a matriarch of the Porter family. Oriented toward the mercantilism and modernism of Salem Town, the Porters did not relish being severed from its congregation. Furthermore, the Porters feared—rightly so—that the Putnams would gain excessive power over the church through their favored minister and, ultimately, over all the towns-people. New England was a theocracy, a religious state: in order to be a full citizen of Salem, you had to be an approved member of its congregation. With their man in the pulpit, the Putnams now had undue influence over who would and would not be welcomed fully into the community.

In addition to these political/religious troubles, there were endless property disputes between members of the two rival families, and these ongoing battles may have added fuel to the witch-hunt fire. Indeed, some historians (those of a particularly conspiratorial mind-set) have suggested that the Putnams actually plotted the demise of Rebecca Nurse and her sisters, prompt-ing their daughter Ann to accuse these women so that the Putnams could ultimately steal their landholdings. Although the existence of such a plot is not out of the question, there is more speculation than actual evidence in support of the idea. (Incidentally, in 1706 the younger Ann Putnam made a public confession for having allowed "a great delusion of Satan" to prompt her to accuse persons she now believed innocent. "I did it not out of any anger, malice, or ill-will to any person, for I had no such thing against one of them, but what I did was [done] ignorantly, being deluded by Satan. And particularly, as I was a chief instrument of accusing of Goodwife Nurse and her two sisters, I desire to lie in the dust, and be humbled for it.")

In recent years, feminist historians have also uncov-ered another dimension to the property disputes in New England—namely, a battle between the sexes. Early in the colony's history, there was a serious

imbalance in the population: the first group of settlers to arrive in Massachusetts Bay consisted primarily of unmarried men. A law passed in the 1630s granted parcels of land (called "maid lots") to unmarried women, as an incentive to lure them to the colony. This gave women the right to own property, but "the land was also, in effect, a dowry—a gift to her future husband—since the community expected these women to marry," as historian Lori Lee Wilson explains it. Another law permitted husbands to will

Officials of the Inquisition strip a suspected witch in preparation for a torture session. Some feminist historians argue that witch-hunts in general, and the Salem episode in particular, had a great deal to do with repressed sexuality and with gender-based resentments.

their property to their widows, and fathers without sons to deed property to their daughters.

The incentive program worked well. By the 1650s, women outnumbered men in the colony, and often operated farms and businesses in direct competition with men. "More and more frequently," Wilson has written, "the charge of witchcraft was leveled at women who had inherited property. Bridget Bishop and Susannah Martin had been accused of witchcraft shortly after their husbands had died and willed them property—prior to 1692. Their accusers were men whose property bordered theirs."

Perhaps Cotton Mather was not wrong to think that the Evil One had come to Salem, but he gravely mistook his form—not the fantastic torments of witchcraft, but the far more mundane and common sins of greed, envy, and vengeance.

There are, of course, many people who still believe that witchcraft is a powerful and effective tool—that there are ways to summon supernatural forces to intervene in human affairs. Considering how many of us believe fervently that an all-powerful God listens to and can answer our prayers, it is perhaps only logical that some percentage of us believe that other occult forces—be they angels, tree spirits, beloved deceased relatives, demons, or Lucifer himself—can also be asked to grant our wishes, hopes, and desires.

Not surprisingly, at least one modern historian has argued that the witch hysteria in Salem in 1692 was ultimately caused by the actual practice of witchcraft. In his 1969 book *Witchcraft at Salem,* Chadwick Hansen examined the trial testimony and essentially took witnesses at their word. He concluded that Bridget Bishop was indeed an effective practitioner of black magic, as were the slaves Candy and Wilmot "Mammy" Redd. According to

Hansen, these women engaged in traditional forms of sorcery: sticking pins in dolls, muttering curses, causing the illnesses and deaths of people who had offended them in some manner. Other women, Hansen claimed, dabbled in such "white magic" practices as fortune-telling and divination. Although the afflicted girls were probably not bewitched so much as caught up in a hysterical fear of becoming bewitched, Hansen argued, their fears were wholly justified.

In Chadwick Hansen, the long-gone Cotton Mather has surely found a 20th-century champion for his views.

Victim of a modern-day witch-hunt? Peggy McMartin Buckey dabs a tear during her trial on child molestation charges. Accusations by a mentally unstable parent fueled hysterical fears that Buckey, co-owner of the McMartin Preschool day-care center in Manhattan Beach, California, and her son, Ray, had horribly abused hundreds of children. After a seven-year ordeal that included two lengthy trials, however, both defendants were released.

Endless Echoes

6

The Salem episode can be viewed as a relatively isolated event, particularly in terms of the bizarre, terrifying, and seemingly inexplicable behavior of the afflicted girls (as well as the boys, men, and women who later joined them in their courtroom fits and denunciations). On the other hand, having examined its specific social and historical setting, one can broaden the perspective across several hundred years in both directions. With the expanded context, a chilling and complex fact is revealed: children have been playing the central role in witch-hunts for several centuries, and they continue to star in modern-day persecution scenarios. Normally considered the innocent victims of adult violence (wars, physical abuse, sexual abuse, and so on), children also turn out to be victimizers more often than we'd like to admit to ourselves.

"Questioning children's innocence is not popular," notes the sociologist Hans Sebald, who has closely examined the critical role of youths in witch panics throughout the centuries.

> In a world that agonizes over perennial betrayal, cruelty, war, mass slaughter, and other failures of humanity, we passionately long for exemplars of unadulterated goodness. The child, like some sacred icon, has been traditionally placed upon an imaginary altar so that we [adults] might revere virtues lacking in ourselves.

Ironically, Sebald goes on to say, when children's behavior doesn't fulfill these sacred expectations, it can cause a severe backlash. The same adults who once romanticized and worshiped the innocence of childhood are most likely to punish youngsters severely if they fall from that state of grace.

Europe in the Middles Ages (roughly from the 5th to the 15th centuries) was ruled by theocracy, just like Puritan New England. The medieval Christian Church claimed to be the infallible authority in all matters concerning good and evil behavior. The strict dualism of sinners and saints pertained to children as well—either they were pure, innocent, idealized souls or they were collaborators with the Devil. Some theologians—even the great Thomas Aquinas—believed it possible for children to be born witches (the progeny of the Devil and a human witch) or for good infants to be replaced with devilish ones immediately after birth by evil midwives. "The moral of the theory was that not every child could be trusted or taken at face value," Sebald writes.

Today, when older children display what we call "behavioral problems," we are apt to attribute it to brain conditions such as attention deficit disorder or to blame it

Thomas Aquinas, the Catholic Church's most prominent medieval theologian, believed that the Devil could mate with human witches. The products of such unions would be witch children who resembled normal infants but who were evil and could never be trusted.

on parental abuse or neglect. Five hundred years ago, the way to explain troublesome children was to label them satanic creatures. Parents put demonological interpretations even on milder forms of childish behavior that we would consider rambunctious but normal. Infants with birth defects such as hydrocephaly (an enlarged head caused by water on the brain) were considered marked by evil and were often abandoned, killed, or allowed to die through neglect.

The need to discipline children with severity had always been a central concept of the European theocracy, but it became even more crucial during the Reformation and Counter-Reformation. The great social, economic, and political upheavals of the time led to much insecurity and anxiety among common people. Which beliefs were correct? Whose teaching should be followed? What was proper behavior for good Christians? In this turmoil, church organizations bore down heavily on their adult flocks to demand righteousness and a sin-free lifestyle, and these adults would in turn bear down heavily on their children. Children bore the brunt of harsh discipline but often rebelled or reacted in subconscious ways. (We usually call such behavior "acting out.") Children's insolent or hostile reactions to such discipline usually provoked adults to crack down even harder.

These developments merged with the growing witch frenzy. During the early stages of the European witch-hunts in the 14th and 15th centuries, the Inquisition targeted organizations more often than individuals. "Heretical" groups—those that preached messages that conflicted with or contradicted official Church teachings—were considered hotbeds of witches and wizards. But over time, as Sebald explains,

> the fear of heretics spread into the private lives of the citizens, where it poisoned interpersonal relationships. Accusations evolved from the inevitable frictions innate in everyday interaction between family members, neighbors, and other people in the community. Common human conditions and emotions, such as ignorance, fear, greed, revenge, and often pure malice, became major catalysts for accusations. It was then that the witch image became a family and neighborhood phenomenon and that children began to assume an important role.

According to the vivid and misogynistic (women-hating) manual for witch-hunters, *Malleus Maleficarum* (The

Hammer of Witches), children were often introduced to the Devil by their mothers or midwives who would ultimately infect whole families. Starting in the 1580s, children became the preferred target of Inquisition investigators. A 1591 manifesto by a German bishop named Peter Binsfield advocated the unconditional credibility (believability) of children's reports, confessions, and denunciations in witchcraft proceedings. Normal criminal procedure exempted minors from torture and capital punishment and barred children's testimony against adults in capital-crime cases. These safeguards were now dropped when it came to witch trials—and children's involvement blossomed.

The vast majority of witch trials up until the 18th century involved children who accused their close relatives, especially their mothers. Children were seen as collaborators of the Devil, but would then become star witnesses for the prosecution against their families. "Possessed" children were subjected to exorcism, but were also pitied for the torments they suffered. They could therefore be encouraged to identify witches, especially close family members, without seeming cruel, ungrateful, or arbitrarily malicious. Many children also voluntarily confessed to witchcraft, and their stories, Hans Sebald writes, "sparkled with a flair for . . . make-believe, the talent to fabricate convincingly and colorfully." Sebald believes that these children often knew they were lying at the start, but eventually came to think their made-up stories were the truth. This phenomenon, called "confabulation," can be observed in people of all ages under the right circumstances of stress or mental illness.

Then, as now, children displayed vivid imaginations—but the products of their imaginations clearly reflected the obsessions and concerns of the adults around them. Sometimes witch stories were generated as a kind of cover for actual crimes of a sexual or familial type, such as incest, concealed pregnancy, abortion, or infanticide. Having relations with the Devil or other witches was a perennial theme in confessions, even among children who were clearly not sexually experienced. Consider, for example, the extensive stories told by "Witchboy," an anonymous young German who dictated his confession to priests in 1629. He speaks of having taken a demon as his "little lover," but then mentions no actual sexual activities other than a single kiss. When facing a confessed witch, inquisitors were in the habit of ferreting out and writing down every dirty sexual detail with voyeuristic glee, and would have done so in this case if the boy had any such actual knowledge to report.

"Not all children failed to give sexual information," Sebald writes.

> On the contrary, some children dwelled on it with great eagerness. . . . This might have been due to actual sexual or erotic experiences, be it through childlike explorations of their own bodies, through relatively harmless experimentation with peers, or through serious sexual involvements. Mostly it was probably due to that fascinating mythomanical tendency of children—as much affliction as talent—to fabricate fantastic stories. The claim of a three-year-old girl that she had sex with the Devil is a blatant instance of such confabulated sexual activity.

If all this sounds eerily familiar, perhaps it's because such storytelling talents have never disappeared entirely from modern culture. The Inquisition was over nearly 400 years ago, but children are still occasionally caught up in a whirlwind drama of sexually charged accusations and confessions.

Make no mistake: child abuse and molestation are very real problems. Indeed, some historians have plausibly suggested that several of the afflicted girls in Salem had been sexually abused by adult males, and that they later assuaged their pain and anguish by unconsciously "projecting" guilt onto other members of the community.

Yet there is also evidence that children, under the right circumstances, are capable of lying about having been victimized. In certain cases, for example, embittered children of divorcing parents have concocted stories about one parent or both, perhaps out of vengeance or perhaps as a way of diverting attention back to themselves. But false accusations are not always this deliberate. Human beings are very suggestible creatures, and children are particularly vulnerable to being influenced by the things they hear and see all around them. Social workers and police officers, charged with investigating possible abuse, often ask so-called leading questions, queries that imply the "right" answer, the answer that the questioner expects. Children generally like to please authority figures by telling them what they want to hear. When parents are anxious about potential abuse by nonrelatives (say, day-care providers or teachers), they may already have a horrific scenario in their mind about what happened. They'll bombard the child with questions, and the child will probably follow their lead. The questioning then turns into, in the words of Hans Sebald, "a veritable rehearsal of a story that the child [begins] to learn by heart." As the story is requested again and again by other authority figures, the child elaborates and provides additional colorful details, but essentially continues to confirm the story first suggested by the adults.

Using a doll, a psychologist interviews two children about sexual abuse. From 17th-century Salem to the present, children's testimony has often proved problematic—particularly when investigators have had preconceived notions about the truth.

We should note that adults are not immune to such suggestibility. In recent cases mature persons, after prolonged interrogations by zealous questioners, have confessed to performing "satanic rituals" involving the rape and murder of children. Although these people were not really tortured in the traditional sense, they may certainly have been "brainwashed" under the sheer stress of being locked in a room and asked the same questions over and over and over again. As with the confessions of yesteryear, modern confessions by alleged satanic practitioners always feature the denunciation of other participants in an imagined conspiracy. But no such confessions have ever been corroborated by any actual physical evidence. "There have, of course, been a number of documented cases of satanic symbolism, many of them in the form of graffiti or in association with delinquent behavior," Sebald points out. "But the use of such symbols is no proof that an organized satanic conspiracy exists."

The media have always been a powerful driving force in witch-hunts. Just as Betty Parris and Abigail Williams most likely read and absorbed stories of possession and bewitchment in books by Cotton Mather and other writers of the day, modern children are quite capable of imitating stories they've picked up on television and in the movies. In a Florida case, a nine-year-old girl gave some utterly convincing testimony that convicted her mother's boyfriend of raping her. Two years later, she admitted that she had fabricated the whole thing after watching an episode of the police drama *21 Jump Street,* in which a rape was described.

The longest and costliest criminal trial in American history began in 1983, when a woman named Judy Johnson accused two teachers at the McMartin Preschool in Manhattan Beach, California, of molesting her son, who was then two and a half years old. A physical exam showed that the boy may have been molested, and from that point on, hysteria swept through the community. Soon 41 children were involved and 208 counts were filed against seven teachers at McMartin. Sixty-three-year-old Peggy Buckey and her son Raymond, 31, were considered the ringleaders of an abuse conspiracy. While the investigation was still under way, Judy Johnson was found to be an acute paranoid schizophrenic and an alcoholic, and she soon died of an alcohol-related liver disease. Nevertheless, as Hans Sebald chronicles, the prosecution continued full steam ahead:

> But by then the prosecution had stirred up enough other witnesses and felt no need to revise [Johnson's] testimony, despite the fact that in retrospect it was considered unreliable. The police had written to two hundred parents stating that they were investigating claims of oral sex and sodomy that presumably had taken place at the school. This disclosure fanned the hysteria and set the stage for more children to come up with lurid tales of abuse. The children were interviewed by [a therapist] who soon established that 369 of the 400 children had been abused. Her technique was highly suggestive: she gave emotional rewards to the children who accused the teachers, and rebuffs to those who did not. "What good are you? You must be dumb," she said to one child who knew nothing about the game 'Naked Movie Star.'

Children were driven around town and asked to point out molesters, a process reminiscent of bringing the Salem girls to Andover. They told fantastic stories —about digging up bodies in cemeteries, being buried alive, seeing teachers fly, and killing animals with bats—that were immediately taken as true. In 1985, the seven teachers (four of whom were members of the Buckey family) were indicted and hauled away in handcuffs in front of a TV camera crew. In January 1986, charges against five of them were dropped when a new district attorney took over the case and declared a complete lack of evidence. But that didn't allay the fears of parents or the suspicions of the community, and Peggy and Raymond Buckey remained in jail until 1990. Their nightmare had lasted seven years.

IN MEMORY OF THOSE INNOCE
WHO DIED DURING THE
SALEM VILLAGE WITCHCRAFT HY
OF 1692

Epilogue:
Salem Today

STERIA

This memorial to the 24 people who died as a result of the Salem witch-hunts stands in the Massachusetts town of Danvers, the site of old Salem Village.

According to a nationwide poll taken in the early 1990s, many Americans retain beliefs in supernatural phenomena. The poll found that 55 percent of Americans firmly believe in the reality of the Devil, 8 percent aren't certain, and the remaining 37 disbelieve. Ten percent of adult Americans believe they have personally talked to, or have heard the voice of, Satan himself. Almost half of all Americans believe that demons sometimes possess humans, nearly 30 percent believe that houses can be haunted, 25 percent believe that ghosts exist and that spirits of dead people can come back to earth. Another significant percentage are "not certain," meaning they haven't ruled out the possibility of such phenomena. Fourteen percent believe that witches really exist. Among teenagers aged 16 to 17, that number rises to 34 percent.

Clearly, the voices of Cotton Mather and other true believers in the "invisible world" are still among us. It's no wonder, then, that large groups of people can be made to believe in satanic ritual abuse without any hard evidence, or that some people have tried to ban the Harry Potter books (make-believe stories about a teenage wizard) from school libraries. The fear of devilish intervention in human affairs continues to obsess at least some part of our population. In the old days, people relied on gossip, folk-tales, old songs, and (if they were literate) religious tracts like *Remarkable Providences* for their understanding of witchcraft and satanism. Once a story made the rounds of the public domain, it generated imitations—whether through suggestibility, fraud, or some combination of the two. Considering how much more pervasive and power-ful our modern mass media is, it may seem surprising that witch panics (or their modern equivalents, such as accusa-tions of satanic ritual abuse) don't happen as often these days as they did 500 years ago.

Furthermore, with the rise of talk shows, "reality programming," and other television formats meant to encourage ordinary people to grab the limelight if they can, modern American culture provides a key ingredient of all demonic possessions or outrageous confessions of witch-craft: an audience. As many historians of witch persecution have noted, afflicted or bewitched children and adults throughout the ages have depended upon the presence of an audience to manifest their symptoms; nobody, as far as we know, experiences devilish fits when they are all by themselves in their bedroom. On the contrary, in Salem and in all similar recorded instances of affliction by witch-craft, a group of concerned and terrified onlookers was an absolute prerequisite. This is not to assert that all such events constitute deliberate "play-acting" on the part of the afflicted, but that human suggestibility and certain kinds

Among certain groups of people, fear of witchcraft and the occult still runs deep, as evidenced by parents' efforts to ban the popular Harry Potter books of J. K. Rowling from school libraries.

of mob behavior arise only in the context of being watched. At your average overhyped teen rock concert, for example, the kids in the front rows (seen by the musicians as well as any TV or video cameras) are far more likely to succumb to hysterical group behavior—screaming, crying, waving their arms, singing along—than are those in the cheap seats, way in the back where no one can see them.

If you have ever experienced the sheer joy of "letting go" at such an event, then you can probably imagine what a triumphant, addictive experience it must have been for those Salem girls to release their hostility against a repressive culture—flinging their Bibles across the room, as Betty Parris did—and, instead of being punished for insolence and bad behavior, being "rewarded" with the terrified compassion of their parents and the entire community. Indeed, when the fit-throwing accusers went to the nearby town of Gloucester, the local people refused to play their role in the drama; they simply turned their backs on the girls. Deprived of the audience structure and feedback they'd grown accustomed to, the group of girls couldn't sustain the proper level of hysteria, and their fits ended immediately.

So with today's ever-present and insatiable audience for extreme phenomena, why don't we have more witch panics? One reason is that secular humanism—the outgrowth of the rationalist philosophies professed by celebrated thinkers like Rousseau and Descartes as well as ordinary men of affairs like Thomas Brattle and Robert Calef—has established itself in our culture as both a counterforce against superstition and a relatively amiable companion to less virulent, more tolerant and ecumenical forms of religious belief and practice. Another important reason we don't see these situations often is that, after Salem, official church doctrine in most parts of America began to separate itself from popular notions of folk magic, and eventually repudiated them altogether. The Reverend Cotton Mather today might be a hugely popular author of a website devoted to nightmarish tales of possession and demonic rituals, or he might be a well-paid consultant to the popular TV drama about paranormal and supernatural phenomena, *The X-Files,* but he would most likely not be a top clergyman at a very powerful and influential church. Or perhaps

A teen idol from the 1970s inspired this scene among his young female audience at a London concert, proving the obvious—that witchcraft isn't the only factor that can produce mass hysteria among children. Some observers assert that an audience often seems to be a prerequisite for such hysteria, however.

he would be—but he'd probably have to keep his more colorful ideas and opinions to himself.

Finally, thanks in part to Increase Mather and his groundbreaking work on evidence, America now has a 300-year-old tradition in our criminal legal system of trying to separate fact from fiction, reliable testimony from gossip and rumor, and hard, objective evidence from mere fantasy. The system is flawed—deeply flawed, some people would argue—and will probably always be so as long as humans are subject to error, zealotry, bad working conditions, low pay, laziness, sloppiness, greed, prejudice, anger, and ambition. But at the very least, as a culture we do make an effort to test and refine the system toward a set of common ideals: to ensure that justice is served, that serious crimes do not go unpunished, that the perpetrators are correctly identified and appropriately sentenced, and that innocent people are, for the most part, left to live their lives in peace.

Salem Village today is now known as Danvers, but the change of name and the turn of three centuries has not dampened the echoes of what happened there. An official Internet site "city guide" of Salem features T. H. Matheson's famous 19th-century oil painting of an accused witch being examined for the Devil's mark. At the Witch Dungeon Museum, the Salem Witch Museum, and the Witch History Museum, dramatic reenactments of various trials take place frequently. Sightseers flock to these sorts of events, while more serious scholars and amatuer sleuths spend hours poring over the 552 original documents about the trial archived at The Peabody Museum.

The place has been a tourist attraction for more than 150 years. In the 1830s, visitors hiked along Gallows Hill (also known as Witch Hill), picking rare wildflowers in the belief that they possessed magical properties. In the early 1900s, a shop in town began selling the first Halloween witch postcards depicting an old crone more fun-loving and grandmotherly than terrifying. Books, plays, and movies about the event have whetted the audience's appetite for more stories about the trials. With the advent of cheap air travel in recent decades, Salem now attracts thousands of visitors from all over the world.

Marked by history, the village is stuck in a perpetual state of performing its past affliction for an ever-growing audience. Modern-day witches—practitioners of the earth-worshipping religious movements also known as Wicca or Paganism—have made Salem a kind of unofficial capital. Modern Wicca witches worship Mother Earth and believe they can harness Her power through meditation and communion with nature. On Halloween night, hundreds of Wiccans come to Salem to hold a candlelight procession and vigil at the Salem Witchcraft Trial Memorial. But many Salem residents believe the memorial to be a sacred space and are offended by its inclusion in what they consider to be an illegitimate religious movement. Wiccan priestess Selena Fox, founder of one of the first legally established Wiccan churches in the country, says, "Three hundred years after the Salem trials, Wiccan witches are still struggling for their rights as a religious and cultural minority in American society. I hope that as present and future generations reflect on the lessons of Salem, that we will all work together for a society that celebrates diversity and truly offers freedom for all."

A self-proclaimed witch named Laurie Cabot moved into town a few decades ago, opened a shop that sells candles, crystals, herbs, incense, and other accoutrements of Wiccan ritual, and eventually became a local celebrity. She wears long black and red robes, sports a pentagram pendant and many rings on her fingers, and favors pale face-powder and dark black mascara. To the superstitious, she is no doubt an intimidating figure. But like many of her colleagues, she spends much of her time defending witchcraft as a venerable, nature-loving, fertility-worshipping, female-oriented practice that offers people an inspiring alternative to more established churches and has nothing to do with the Devil. Not everyone is inclined to believe her, or to respect her notoriety. In the early 1980s, over the objections of many local residents, Massachusetts governor Michael Dukakis named Cabot the Official Witch of Salem—but the city mayor has refused to grant the title officially.

Three hundred years later, the ghost of Cotton

A student at Laurie Cabot's Witch Shoppe in Salem, Massachusetts. Today devotees of Wicca, a modern belief system that incorporates elements of witchcraft, have made Salem their unofficial capital.

Mather still whispers terrible scenarios of bewitchment and devilry in the ears of some of Salem's people. When these folks pass Laurie Cabot on the street, they avert their eyes, genuinely afraid that with a mere glance, this woman can stain their innocent souls and engulf them in a wave of pure evil.

Chronology

1620   The Pilgrims—English Puritans who have separated from the Church of England—land at Plymouth Rock and found the Massachusetts Bay Colony

1630   John Winthrop is elected the first governor of the newly chartered colony of Massachusetts (corresponding to most of present-day Massachusetts and New Hampshire) and sails there with the first group of Puritan immigrants

1672   The men of Salem Village receive permission to form a meetinghouse and hire a preacher

1689   After 25 years of disputes and disagreements over three successive preachers at Salem Village, the church is formed and new arrival Samuel Parris is ordained

1692   *January:* Betty Parris and Abigail Williams first exhibit a mysterious affliction with symptoms such as blasphemous screaming, convulsive seizures, trance-like states, and spells

February: Tituba and John Indian bake "witch cake" with the girls' urine and feed it to a dog; other girls in the neighborhood, including Ann Putnam and Elizabeth Hubbard, also start having fits; they accuse Tituba, Sarah Good, and Sarah Osborne of being witches and of tormenting them

March: Of the three accused witches first examined by the magistrates, only Tituba confesses; later in the month, Martha Corey and Rebecca Nurse are accused, examined, and imprisoned; Ann Putnam and Gertrude Pope, two adult women, join the afflicted girls; Sarah Good's young daughter Dorcas is accused, examined, and sent to prison

April: By the end of the month, 23 more residents, including John and Elizabeth Proctor, Giles Corey, and Bridget Bishop, are in jail

May: George Burroughs, former preacher of Salem Village, is arrested and brought back from his new home in Maine; Governor William Phips and Increase Mather arrive from England with a new provincial charter; by the end of the month, at least 39 more people are in jail

June: Phips appoints a Court of Oyer and Terminer to try the accused witches; Bridget Bishop, the first to be convicted, is hanged on the 10th; one of the judges, Nathan Saltonstall, resigns from the bench, outraged

Chronology

over the use of spectral evidence and other disturbing aspects of the trial; the arrests and examinations continue and spill over into Andover, Ipswich, Gloucester, and other areas; five more Salem witches are tried and convicted

July: Sarah Good, Rebecca Nurse, Susannah Martin, Elizabeth Howe, and Sarah Wildes are hanged on Gallows Hill

August: George Burroughs, John and Elizabeth Proctor, John Willard, George Jacobs, and Martha Carrier are tried, convicted, and sentenced to hang; Elizabeth Proctor is spared on account of her pregnancy

September: Fifteen more are tried, convicted, and sentenced; five of the convicted are spared, one because she is pregnant and four because they confess, but the rest are hanged; Giles Corey refuses to testify and is pressed to death

October: The girls start to name several prominent people, including Lady Phips and the wife of Increase Mather, as witches, and a backlash begins; heeding the opinion of his colleagues who decry the trials, Increase Mather writes *Cases of Conscience,* which casts serious doubt on the validity of spectral evidence; Thomas Brattle writes his open letter criticizing the trials; Phips halts the process, then formally dissolves the Court of Oyer and Terminer

1693   With no more spectral evidence to rely on, the jurors convict only three of the remaining accused witches; Phips reprieves them, along with five others previously sentenced; eventually Phips orders the release of all accused witches remaining in jail, on payment of their fees

Further Reading

Boyer, Paul, and Stephen Nissenbaum. *Salem Possessed: The Social Origins of Witchcraft*. Cambridge, Mass.: Harvard University Press, 1974.

Breslaw, Elaine G. *Tituba, Reluctant Witch of Salem: Devilish Indians and Puritan Fantasies*. New York: NYU Press, 1996.

Hill, Frances. *The Salem Witch Trials Reader*. New York: DaCapo Press, 2000.

Hoffer, Peter Charles. *The Devil's Disciples: Makers of the Salem Witchcraft Trials*. Baltimore: Johns Hopkins Press, 1996.

Sebald, Hans. *Witch-Children: From Salem Witch-Hunts to Modern Courtrooms*. Amherst, N.Y.: Prometheus Books, 1995.

Wilson, Lori Lee. *How History Is Invented: The Salem Witch Trials*. Minneapolis, Minn.: Lerner Publications, 1997.

Index

Index

Picture Credits

SANDY ASIRVATHAM, a graduate of Columbia University with a B.A. in Philosophy & Economics and a M.F.A. in Writing, is a journalist, creative writer, and aspiring musician living in Baltimore. As a professional writer for over 10 years, she has written on a variety of cultural, political, and artistic topics. Her other books for Chelsea House include biographies of actor Bruce Willis and tennis star Venus Williams, and a history of the police in America. This is her first time writing about the Salem witch trials.

JILL McCAFFREY has served for four years as national chairman of the Armed Forces Emergency Services of the American Red Cross. Ms. McCaffrey also serves on the board of directors for Knollwood—the Army Distaff Hall. The former Jill Ann Faulkner, a Massachusetts native, is the wife of Barry R. McCaffrey, formerly a member of President Bill Clinton's cabinet and director of the White House Office of National Drug Control Policy. The McCaffreys are the parents of three grown children: Sean, a major in the U.S. Army; Tara, an intensive care nurse and captain in the National Guard; and Amy, a seventh-grade teacher. The McCaffreys also have two grandchildren, Michael and Jack.